AUSCHWITZ

Voices From the Death Camp

The Holocaust Through Primary Sources

James M. Deem

Enslow Publishers, Inc.
40 Industrial Road
Box 398
Berkeley Heights, NJ 07922
USA

http://www.enslow.com

Library of Congress Cataloging-in-Publication Data

   Deem, James M.

    Auschwitz : voices from the death camp / James M. Deem.

      p. cm. — (The Holocaust through primary sources)

    Includes bibliographical references and index.

    Summary: "Examines Auschwitz, a death camp during the Holocaust, including its construction and daily workings, true accounts from prisoners of the camp and Nazi perpetrators, and how more than 1 million people were murdered there"—Provided by publisher.

    ISBN 978-0-7660-3322-1

    1. Auschwitz (Concentration camp)—Juvenile literature. 2. Holocaust, Jewish (1939–1945)—Juvenile literature. 3. Jews—Persecutions—Europe—Juvenile literature. I. Title.

    D805.5.A96D44 2011

    940.53'180922—dc22

2010003064

Paperback ISBN 978-1-59845-346-1

Printed in China

052011 Leo Paper Group, Heshan City, Guangdong, China

10 9 8 7 6 5 4 3 2 1

To Our Readers: We have done our best to make sure all Internet Addresses in this book were active and appropriate when we went to press. However, the author and the publisher have no control over and assume no liability for the material available on those Internet sites or on other Web sites they may link to. Any comments or suggestions can be sent by e-mail to comments@enslow.com or to the address on the back cover.

Every effort has been made to locate all copyright holders of material used in this book. If any errors or omissions have occurred, please contact us at www.enslow.com. We will try to make corrections in future editions.

For text permission credit lines, please see p. 123.

Illustration Credits: Archive of the Auschwitz-Birkenau State Museum, pp. 17, 44, 48, 52–53, 60, 74, 101; Archive of the Auschwitz-Birkenau State Museum / The Archives of the Institute of National Remembrance, Poland, p. 36; Associated Press, p. 80; Enslow Publishers, Inc., p. 12; Getty Images, p. 19; Courtesy of James M. Deem, pp. 113, 114; © Lebrecht Music & Arts / The Image Works, p. 8; Courtesy of Paweł Sawicki, pp. 14, 43, 85; Courtesy of the Primo Levi Family, p. 96; © Simon Shepheard / Impact / HIP / The Image Works, p. 62; ullstein bild / The Granger Collection, New York, p. 58; USHMM, courtesy of Anna and Joshua Heilman, pp. 87, 92, 94; USHMM, courtesy of anonymous donor, pp. 28, 41; USHMM, courtesy of Archiwum Dokumentacji Mechanicznej, p. 64; USHMM, courtesy of Belarussian State Archive of Documentary Film and Photography, p. 103; USHMM, courtesy of Bruna D'Urbino, pp. 110–111; USHMM, courtesy of Charles and Hana Bruml, p. 98; USHMM, courtesy of Hava Shaked, p. 73; USHMM, courtesy of Instytut Pamieci Narodowej, pp. 10, 31, 51, 70, 71; USHMM, courtesy of Jacquelyn Gervay, p. 107; USHMM, courtesy of Joseph Maier, p. 35; USHMM, courtesy of Morris Rosen, p. 22; USHMM, courtesy of National Archives and Records Administration, pp. 38, 77; USHMM, courtesy of Panstwowe Muzeum with Oświęcim-Brzezinka, p. 89; USHMM, courtesy of Philip Vock, p. 25; USHMM, courtesy of Yad Vashem, pp. 6, 67, 82; Yad Vashem Photo Archives, pp. 56, 105.

Cover Illustration: USHMM, courtesy of Yad Vashem (Jewish women and children walk toward the gas chambers after having been selected for death in Auschwitz-Birkenau in May 1944); USHMM, courtesy of Fritz Gluckstein (Star of David artifact).

Contents

INTRODUCTION

In May 1944, Olga Lengyel went to the Cluj, Hungary, train station with her husband, Miklos, and their family. A prominent Jewish doctor, Miklos had been accused by German authorities, who now controlled Hungary, of refusing to use German-produced drugs in his medical practice; he was told that, as punishment, he was to be deported to Germany. Olga and her parents decided to join Miklos on the deportation train; the couple's young sons would come, too.

But when the family arrived at the station, Olga found a train of cattle cars, many already crammed with Jews from Cluj and other Hungarian towns. Olga and her family were shoved into a car with ninety others, confined to a space that would have held only eight horses.[1] The Germans had lied to them.

During the seven-day journey that followed, the passengers were given no food and almost no water. Half of the people in Olga's car had no room to sit. A few families had brought chamber pots, and these became makeshift toilets in one corner of the car. When they were full, the pots were emptied out of a small window—the only window in the car.

On the second day, a man died of a heart attack; when the train stopped at the next station, the guards told the dead man's son to "Keep your corpse. You will have many more of them soon!"[2]

On the third day, a guard shouted through the window at one station, "Thirty wristwatches, right away. If not, you may all consider yourselves dead!"[3] Olga's son, Thomas, gave up the wristwatch he had been given in third grade.

The guard returned, demanding fountain pens and briefcases. The third time, he promised that, if the passengers gave him their jewelry, he would bring them some water, the first they had been offered on the trip. When the jewelry had been collected, a bucket of water was lowered into the car. But many of the passengers did not get a drop.

During the next four days, more people died from disease, from heat, from thirst, from hunger. On the seventh day, the train reached its final destination. When the train door was finally opened, the trainload of Jews had no idea where they were. Confused and frightened, they were ordered out of the cattle cars by German soldiers. Men were told to stand in one line; women and children in another. Olga saw thousands of Jewish passengers standing on the platform. Nearby, emaciated men in striped prison uniforms took their belongings from the train. Next, the men removed the corpses from each car.

A group of German officers began to separate the passengers further. Some—the children, the elderly, the sick, the disabled— were sent to the left. Everyone else was waved to the right. Anyone who complained was beaten immediately until he or she complied.

When it was Olga's turn, she was motioned to the right with her mother. Thomas was sent to the left. But the German officer hesitated when he saw Olga's other son, Arvad.

Jewish women and children deported from Hungary wait in line at Auschwitz after being separated from the men in May 1944. Olga Lengyel went through this process when she arrived at Auschwitz with her family.

"This boy must be more than twelve," the officer told Olga.[4]

Thinking that the children's line might receive special care, she told the officer that Arvad was not yet that old. The officer sent Arvad to the left. Now that her sons seemed to be safe in the group on the left, Olga asked if her mother could change lines to help care for her sons. The officer agreed.

Then the line on the left was marched away, unaware of what would happen next. It was only later—after she was shorn of her hair, searched, disinfected, and dressed in old clothes—that Olga learned where she was. She and her family had been taken to Auschwitz, a concentration camp in German-occupied Poland that had become a death camp for Jews and others that the Nazis considered undesirable. After they left the train platform, Olga's sons and parents had been taken to a gas chamber and killed with everyone else in the left-hand line.

The Beginning of Auschwitz

Auschwitz, as it was known in Germany (or Oświęcim in Poland), was selected to be a concentration camp in February 1940, some five months after Germany invaded Poland to begin World War II. Nazi officials thought an old Polish military camp on the outskirts of town would provide a good foundation for *konzentrationslager* (or KL) Auschwitz.[5]

On April 30, 1940, Rudolf Höss, the first commandant of KL-Auschwitz, arrived to remodel the run-down barracks. At first, KL-Auschwitz was intended to be a short-term holding camp for Polish political prisoners before they were shipped off to other camps.[6] The purpose, however, changed almost immediately as more prisoners arrived. In short order, it became a work camp primarily for Polish political prisoners. By March 1941, almost 11,000 Polish prisoners were housed there. By the end of 1941, after the arrival of Soviet prisoners of war (POWs), the prisoner population was about 18,000.[7]

This is a postcard with a view of the old town in Oświęcim, or Auschwitz, at the beginning of the twentieth century.

Auschwitz I:
The Administrative Center

Auschwitz I was the original camp and administrative center. Prisoners entered this camp under a large iron gateway that said: *Arbeit Macht Frei* ("Work will set you free"). At first, Polish prisoners were housed there in barracks (called blocks). They added second stories to the one-story barracks and built additional blocks to house an increasing number of prisoners. But there were no rewards for the labor, which was required in all types of weather. Although the death of a prisoner was not the intended result at first, some prisoners did die from natural causes, from brutal punishment, or from the harsh conditions in which they were forced to live. Their bodies were incinerated in a small crematorium within the camp proper.

The most-feared barrack was Block 11, the jail. There, prisoners receiving punishment were often placed in cramped basement cells and deprived of food. Prisoners sentenced to death were executed by gun in the courtyard between Block 10 and Block 11, usually against the so-called Black Wall.

In September 1941, camp officials decided to experiment with a new method of execution, a poison gas called Zyklon B; they gassed a group of Soviet POWs in the basement of Block 11 with the new poison. When that proved successful, a larger group of some nine hundred Soviet POWs were gassed in the crematorium (now called Crematorium I) and their bodies were burned in the adjacent ovens.[8]

These experiments showed the Nazi officials that the gas chamber could effectively kill people on a mass scale. When small transports of Jews began to arrive at the camp later in the fall of 1941, they were gassed in the crematorium.[9] As the transports grew larger, however, the Germans faced two problems: First, the crematorium could only burn about 340 bodies a day, and second, it was located too near the prisoners' barracks making it difficult to keep their mass murders secret.[10]

These two problems would be eliminated when Nazi officials decided to expand Auschwitz.

A view of the iron gateway at Auschwitz I that the prisoners entered through when arriving at the camp.

Auschwitz II: The Death Camp

In October 1941, Heinrich Himmler, the leader of the *Schutzstaffel* (SS), ordered the creation of an even larger sub-camp, named Auschwitz-Birkenau, almost two miles from Auschwitz I. It was to be built on the site of a small Polish village named Brzezinka (Birkenau, in German). The Nazis had evicted the residents and razed most of the buildings; then they forced Soviet POWs to build the new camp.

Auschwitz II would eventually become the largest Nazi concentration camp, housing some 200,000 prisoners.[11] At the beginning of 1942, when the first transport of Jewish prisoners arrived, KL-Auschwitz developed a clear second purpose: Auschwitz II became a full-time killing center, or death camp, where hundreds of thousands of Jews were systematically executed upon their arrival.

At Auschwitz II, more barracks were built to handle the growing number of eastern European Jews, Roma and Sinti (commonly known as "Gypsies"), and others that the Germans considered undesirable. So many Jews were expected in trainloads of cattle cars that the railroad line was extended to the center of the camp in 1944. When a transport of Jewish prisoners arrived, a life and death "selection" was usually made. If it occurred, the old, the young, the weak, women with children, and the sick were separated and marched unknowingly to their immediate deaths. Told to undress so that they could take a shower, they were then escorted by guards into the shower room. Once inside, the guards left, and the doors were closed. The sealed room was then filled with gas, killing everyone inside.

Prisoners who were not selected for death were taken to other areas of the camp where they were forced to work under terrible conditions, until they often died of starvation, disease, or beatings from the guards.

Auschwitz II: Gas Chambers

In March 1942, Auschwitz II had only one small gas chamber, Bunker 1. This bunker, also known as "The Little Red House" for its redbrick exterior, was formerly a farm cottage in Brzezinka that had been converted into a two-room killing chamber.[12]

NAZI CAMPS IN OCCUPIED EUROPE

0   250 Miles

0   250KM

1944 International Boundaries
- German-Occupied
- German Ally
- Liberated/Allies
- Neutral Countries
- Historical Poland
- ○ Concentration, forced labor, transit camps
- ● Death camps

Auschwitz was the largest concentration camp established by the Nazis. Between 1933 and 1945, the Nazis built about twenty thousand camps and Auschwitz was one of six death camps. This map shows some of the larger Nazi camps during the Holocaust.

Prisoners undressed in two nearby barracks, then entered the "little red house." Next, German SS guards dropped poison gas pellets into the rooms, killing the victims. About eight hundred people could be gassed at one time.[13] Not long after, a larger bunker, named Bunker 2 or "the little white house," was opened. It had four rooms, which could accommodate some twelve hundred gassing victims at one time.[14]

But the problem for the Nazis was that both houses did not contain ovens for burning the victims' remains. Bodies had to be removed from the buildings and cremated in nearby open pits, a process that the Nazis found tedious and time-consuming. A special prisoner work detail, called the *Sonderkommando*, was begun to prepare the victims for gassing and to dispose of their bodies afterward.

In 1943, both farmhouses were replaced by four large factory-like buildings that combined gas chambers and crematoria. Crematoria II and III were somewhat smaller and had two floors. Because the gas chambers were located in the basement, the Sonderkommando had to move the bodies to the furnaces on the ground floor above. Crematoria IV and V, in a removed area close to Bunkers 1 and 2, improved upon II and III by placing the gas chambers and furnaces on the same floor, making the work of the Sonderkommando more efficient. In all, these four buildings could kill approximately 4,400 people every day or 120,000 people each month.[15]

This photo shows the inside of a gas chamber at Auschwitz I after the camp was liberated in January 1945.

Auschwitz III: Slave Labor Camps

Auschwitz III was a series of sub-camps where prisoners worked as slaves in factories to produce synthetic rubber, munitions, and other items necessary for the war. In all there were some forty factory camps.[16] The command center and the largest camp by far—with ten thousand prisoners (mostly Jewish)—was the Buna camp in the town of Monowitz (Monowice in Polish).[17] These sub-camps helped fund the war. Major German corporations paid the SS for slave laborers; the money was then deposited in the Nazi treasury.[18]

The End of Auschwitz

Near the end of November 1944, the Soviet army began to close in on Auschwitz. Heinrich Himmler ordered the SS at Auschwitz to stop all gassings and begin the destruction of the crematoria.[19] Although Crematorium V was still used to cremate the bodies of prisoners who died of "natural causes," by the time the Soviet army arrived at the end of January 1945, the four crematoria were in ruins.

The camp was also mostly empty, having been evacuated by the SS. Most of the surviving prisoners were forced to march in freezing weather to other concentration camps. Many who could not keep up were shot and killed. In the end, most of the people sent to Auschwitz died without leaving a trace.

No one knows for certain the exact number of people killed there. Using various documents that survived the war (reports and even telegrams, for example), researchers calculate that at least 1,305,000 people were taken to the camp. This number includes:

- 1,095,000 European Jews
- 147,000 Poles
- 23,000 "Gypsies" (Roma and Sinti)
- 15,000 Soviet POWs
- 25,000 other prisoners[20]

But estimating the number of people who died there is more difficult. Nazi officials at the camp did maintain death certificates for registered prisoners, but not all prisoners were registered.

Beginning in March 1943, none of the Jews transported to Auschwitz and selected for immediate death in the gas chambers were registered. Other executed prisoners were also never recorded on prisoner rolls.

Still, by determining how many Auschwitz prisoners were transferred to other camps (some 213,000), how many escaped (about 500), and how many survived when the camp was liberated in 1945 (about 8,000), researchers have concluded that at least 1.1 million people must have met their deaths at Auschwitz.[21]

1 Kazimierz Albin

I n June 1940, barely a month after KL-Auschwitz had opened, a seventeen-year-old Polish youth named Kazimierz Albin was on the first large prisoner transport to the camp. He had been arrested in Slovakia five months earlier when he tried to make his way to France and join the Polish Army. The army had regrouped there after the German invasion of Poland in September 1939.

At first, Kazimierz was held by the Slovakian police, but when he learned that he would be handed over to the German Gestapo, Kazimierz escaped. Captured and rearrested, he was jailed by the Gestapo and sent by train with 727 other prisoners to Auschwitz.

In Tarnów, Poland, Polish political prisoners await for their transport to Auschwitz. Kazimierz Albin was on the first large transport to the camp.

Arrival in Auschwitz

When the train arrived, Kazimierz was terrified by what he observed:

> [W]e saw extended lines of armed SS-men on either side of the track. The carriage doors were thrown open. . . . Our escorts, who up until now had been relatively calm, suddenly started on us as if possessed. Using their rifle butts, they shoved us out of the carriage and, amid ear-splitting shouts, drove us through a gate into a large square surrounded by a thick barbed-wire fence. At every corner, perched on tall wooden beams, was a watchtower with a machine gun manned by SS-men.[1]

Besides the SS officers, he noticed a small group of other men. They were dressed in blue-and-white striped uniforms and wore caps. Kazimierz thought that they looked like sailors. Then, an SS officer gave a command, and the groups of "sailors" turned to face the newly arrived prisoners.

> We now saw their suntanned faces, their sadistically taut lips, and the spiteful gleam in their eyes, all of which bode no good. There were green triangles on their shirts and trousers, and beneath them each had a number between 1 and 30.

> *A moment later, bats and whips, pulled out from their trousers, were whirling in the air. Already swaying from exhaustion, we were now subjected to a severe beating from these thugs.*[2]

What Kazimierz did not know then was that these thirty "sailors" were also prisoners, sent from other German concentration camps to become the first *kapo*, or prisoner guards, at Auschwitz. German by birth, many of the kapos became notorious for their brand of cruel and sometimes deadly punishment.

An original uniform from Auschwitz. Kazimierz Albin received this type of uniform and prisoner number when he arrived at Auschwitz.

Kazimierz and the other new prisoners had their heads shaved and were told to take showers. Next they were each handed a card bearing a number. Kazimierz was given Number 118. He was the 118th prisoner at Auschwitz.

A Deadly Warning and Initiation

Shortly afterward, the new prisoners were reassembled in the main square. There an SS officer addressed them:

This is Auschwitz concentration camp. As an enemy of the German people you will be interned here until the end of the war. . . . For resisting authority or attempted to escape, the penalty is death. The young and the healthy will live for no longer than three months. . . . The only exit out of here is through the crematorium chimney.[3]

Early the next morning, the prisoners were sent outside for a brutal session of exercise. The kapos and the SS officers commanded the prisoners to run in place, to march, and then, for their amusement, to squat, to hop, to waddle, to roll, to run again and again across the assembly square. Since many of the prisoners were sick or weak before coming to Auschwitz, they could not keep up with the commands. As a result, they were beaten; many were unconscious by the time they were allowed to eat.

THE KAPOS

At Auschwitz, most prisoners feared the kapos as much as they feared the SS guards.

The first thirty prisoners to become kapos were sent to Auschwitz on May 5, 1940. They were placed in charge of the Polish political prisoners, a group they detested. In this way, the SS made certain that the kapos would take whatever steps necessary for their orders to be fulfilled.

Heinrich Himmler, head of the SS, described a kapo this way:

> *His job is to see that the work gets done . . . thus he has to push his men. As soon as we are no longer satisfied with him, he is no longer a kapo, and returns to the other inmates. He knows that they will beat him to death his first night back. . . . Since we don't have enough Germans here, we use others—of course a French kapo for Poles, a Polish kapo for Russians; we play one nation against another.*[4]

When the synthetic rubber plant at Monowitz had to be built quickly, SS officers abused the kapos who in turn punished the prisoners in their work detail. Rudolf Vrba, an Auschwitz survivor, recalled a scene at Monowitz: "The S.S. man would kick viciously at the kapo and roar, 'Get these swine moving, you lazy oaf. Don't you know that wall's to be finished by eleven o'clock?' The kapo would scramble to his feet, pound into the prisoners, lashing them on, faster, faster, faster."[5]

Women, too, were kapos of female work groups. The larger the camp grew, the more the SS relied on the kapos to control the prisoners.[6]

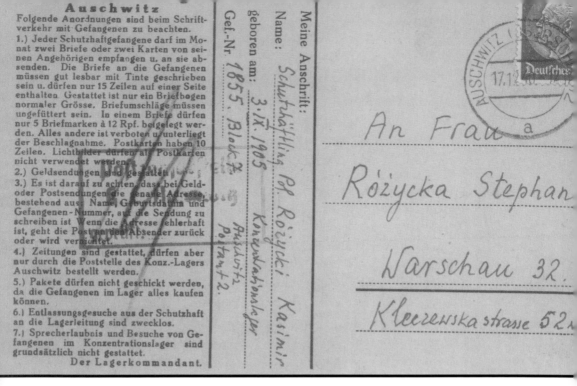

The Polish prisoners in Auschwitz suffered under extremely brutal conditions. In the early days of the camp, prisoners could still send and receive mail. This is a postcard sent by a Polish prisoner, Kasimir Rozycki, to his wife, Stephania, on December 17, 1940. At left of the postcard are the rules about sending and receiving mail in the camp.

That afternoon, the kapos had determined that a few Polish Jews were in the ranks of the 728 prisoners. As the non-Jewish prisoners performed their exercises, the Jews were given even crueler ones so that "after a while we had to carry them bloody and unconscious to the well."[7]

For six days, the routine was the same. The exercises were so intense that some older prisoners began to die; the younger ones, like Kazimierz, were ready to collapse from exhaustion.[8] Only when another transport of three hundred prisoners arrived on June 20 were the prisoners spared from the exercises. The kapos and officers focused instead on the new arrivals.

The Escape of Number 220

By July 6, the camp population had grown to about 1,500 prisoners. During the evening roll call that day, all prisoners were accounted for—except for Number 220. This was the first time that a prisoner had gone missing, and camp officials were not pleased.

That day, Number 220 had been part of a *kommando,* or work group, assigned to clear the camp canals that led to a nearby river. All of the workers on that kommando were called away and beaten, their cries heard by the assembled prisoners. When they did not reveal any information, the prisoners who slept in the same room as Number 220 were taken away and brutally interrogated.

Finally, desperate to know what happened to Number 220, the camp commandant, Rudolf Höss, told the remaining prisoners that, if anyone who knew about the escape did not come forward, all inmates would be beaten.

> We all just stood there . . . in total silence and completely terrified. No one moved. After a while [Höss] gave the signal and the SS-men immediately ploughed into our ranks, throwing punches left, right and centre and felling prisoners with powerful kicks, while the Kapos followed on behind them and restored order to the columns with their bull-whips. . . .

> *The mere fact that we were not allowed to move from the spot was torture in itself. Eventually a prisoner was forced to empty his bladder or bowels where he stood and when that happened he was naturally subjected to further physical and verbal abuse.*[9]

The SS and the kapos left the prisoners standing at roll call overnight. Many collapsed from exhaustion and dehydration. At two o'clock the next afternoon, eleven prisoners were sent to the basement of Block 13. The remaining prisoners were allowed to return to their barracks.

A Decision to Escape

Over the next two years, Kazimierz witnessed many other escapes. Even though prisoners were often punished for others' attempts, Kazimierz noted that "every successful escape gave us a sense of satisfaction and raised our spirits."[10]

By the time he turned twenty, on August 30, 1942, Kazimierz decided that he would celebrate his next birthday far away from KL-Auschwitz. He and a small group of other prisoners planned to run away in early May. In preparation, Kazimierz practiced reading the constellations in the night sky so that he would be able to locate the polestar (North Star) and use it as a compass.

Kazimierz Albin and his friend Franek had to crawl under the barbed-wire fence at Auschwitz in order to make their escape.

On the evening of February 27, 1943, however, Kazimierz and a friend named Franek discovered that another group of prisoners also intended to escape later that night. They feared that their escape plans might be ruined so the two decided to leave immediately.

Wearing dark blue boiler suits, the two men eluded notice as they ran though the well-lit area leading to the camp's barbed-wire fence. The men crawled under the wire, crossed a road, and arrived at a nearby river. Suddenly, the camp siren sounded, alerting the guards of their escape.

A Successful Ending

Using the stars that he had studied, Kazimierz determined the proper direction for their escape. But the approaching search parties with their barking dogs caused Franek to become confused and fearful. He urged Kazimierz to run in another direction. For a while, Kazimierz agreed until they were surrounded by SS men shooting flares.

Finally, Kazimierz took the lead and, guided by the polestar, then by Orion, the two eluded the searchers. By the time the stars disappeared in the morning light, the men had reached a barn where they could spend the day. During the next few weeks, helped by many people, they made their way to Krakow, Poland, Kazimierz's hometown. For the rest of the war, he lived there under an assumed name and helped the Polish resistance against the Nazis.

2 Rudolf Höss

udolf Höss, the commandant of KL-Auschwitz, supervised its creation and daily operation for many years. He was proud of turning the camp into "the largest human killing center in all of history."[1] After the war, he was arrested and sentenced to death for the many war crimes he committed. During his trial, Höss wrote an account, which outlined portions of his life, including his time at KL-Auschwitz.

Becoming a Killer

Born into a devout Catholic family in Baden-Baden, Germany, Höss turned away from his faith as a teenager, when a priest betrayed his confidence. During confession, he told his priest that he had pushed a boy down the stairs at school and caused him to break an ankle. Although church law forbade the priest to tell anyone what Rudolf had done, he revealed the deed to Höss's strict father. Höss was promptly punished.

Soon after, Höss faced a personal tragedy when his father died suddenly. Around the same time, World War I began, and although he was only fourteen, Höss joined the German army. By seventeen, he had been awarded numerous medals and was the youngest noncommissioned officer in the army. The next year, World War I was over. But he faced another personal tragedy when he returned home and found that his mother had died, his family home had been sold, and their possessions divided among greedy relatives.[2] His mother's dying hope was that Höss would take up the priesthood.

Instead, he joined a private military organization and left his relatives and Catholic faith behind. By the time he was twenty-two, Höss had met Adolf Hitler and become a member of the Nazi Party. Willing to do whatever was necessary for his political beliefs, he helped some friends kill a teacher that they thought had betrayed them. They took the man "into the nearby forest, beat and bludgeoned him, slit his throat, and finally shot him twice in the head."[3] Höss was arrested as the ringleader and sentenced to ten years in prison, but he was released after serving only a little more than four years.

Rudolf Höss, center, in Auschwitz in 1944. Höss joined the SS in 1934 and became a concentration camp guard.

A Concentration Camp Career

In 1934, Heinrich Himmler, the head of the SS (a military organization loyal to Hitler), and an acquaintance, encouraged him to join the SS and become a guard at the Dachau concentration camp near Munich. Although he preferred to be a soldier, Höss accepted the position. Six months later he was promoted to block leader against his wishes. When he asked to be reassigned to his former position, the SS officer in charge refused; Höss gave in. As he explained:

> I accepted my fate, which I had voluntarily chosen, even though deep inside I quietly hoped to find another kind of duty in the service in the future. At that time, however, this was unthinkable because [his superior officer] said I was very much suited for prison duty.[4]

After four years, he was sent to Sachsenhausen concentration camp near Berlin, Germany. He became an assistant to the camp commander, a much more important job. There, he learned even more about the management of concentration camps. He was also in charge of several executions, including another SS officer— a friend of Höss—who had accidentally allowed a prisoner to escape.

Incensed, Himmler ordered the man's immediate execution. As Höss recalled:

> *The condemned man was a decent person in his middle thirties, married with three children, who had been conscientious and loyal in his duties. . . . He went to his death calm and collected. To this day I still cannot understand how I could have calmly given the order to fire.*[5]

In May 1940, Höss was appointed commandant of the newly established KL-Auschwitz. His job was to take the old camp and make it suitable for ten thousand prisoners.[6] He knew it would be easier to build a new camp, but he followed his orders. Before he could begin to remodel the camp, however, the first prisoners began to arrive.

Gassing the Prisoners

For the first year, Polish political prisoners were the main inmates of Auschwitz. Many were executed by pistol along the Black Wall of Block 11. In July 1941, they were joined by a transport of Soviet prisoners of war. Taken to Block 11, they were killed within a few days of their arrival.[7]

But Höss had another plan for the next transport of 600 POWs. He had already experimented with a more efficient method of execution: poison gas. When the transport arrived, the Soviet POWs, along with about 250 sick Polish political prisoners, were placed in the basement of Block 11 and locked in.

This is the entrance to the gas chamber, Crematorium I, in Auschwitz, where the Nazis tested Zyklon B to murder Soviet prisoners of war.

Then Zyklon B, gas-producing crystals that officials had used to exterminate rats and lice from the camp, were poured into the basement.

Although the gas worked, it was difficult to remove the fumes from the basement afterward. So Höss tried another gassing, this time on 900 Soviet POWs in the camp's mortuary (now known as Crematorium I). Told that they would be deloused, they undressed and walked into the chamber. The doors were closed behind them, and the Zyklon B pellets were dropped into the mortuary through holes punched into the ceiling.

Höss recalled the scene when the mortuary doors were opened afterward:

> *There for the first time I saw gassed bodies in mass. Even though I imagined death by gas to be much worse, I was still overcome by a sick feeling, a horror. I always imagined death by gas a terrible choking suffocation, but the bodies showed no signs of convulsions. . . . At the time I really didn't waste any thoughts about the killing of Russian POWs. It was ordered; I had to carry it out. But I must admit . . . that the gassings had a calming effect on me, since in the near future the mass annihilation of the Jews was to begin. Up to this point it was not clear to me . . . how the killing of the expected masses was to be done. . . . Now I was at ease.*[8]

The Killing Machine: Auschwitz Birkenau

In order to carry out the mass murder of the Jews, Rudolf Höss needed to select a proper site where larger gas chambers could be constructed:

> We decided that a peasant farmstead situated in the north-west corner of what later became the third building sector at Birkenau would be the most suitable. It was isolated and screened by woods and hedges, and it was also not far from the railway. The bodies could be placed in long, deep pits dug in the nearby meadows. We had not at that time thought of burning the corpses.[9]

THE "FINAL SOLUTION"

In the years leading up to World War II, the Nazi Party enacted laws and policies in Germany that were intended to create "a racially pure, physically perfect people," which the Nazis referred to as the "Aryan race."[10] These laws discriminated against the Jews of Germany and forced many to leave the country. As the Nazis gained more power, they considered the possibility of deporting all remaining Jews outside of the German state. Shortly after the start of World War II, Nazi officials even considered forcing Jews to live on a reservation in Russia, if they were able to defeat Russia and seize its land.[11]

Instead, the Nazis chose to build a number of "extermination centers." Auschwitz became one, in part because of its ideal central location on railroad lines connecting eastern and western Europe. The gas chambers at Auschwitz allowed the Nazis to achieve one of their main goals: "the Final Solution to the Jewish question."[12] This term, used by the Nazis, was a secret way of discussing the genocide, or the mass killing, of European Jews. Auschwitz commandant Rudolf Höss was told about the "final solution" sometime in 1941. As Heinrich Himmler explained, "All the Jews within our reach must be annihilated during this war."[13]

When the first Birkenau gas chamber was in use, Höss observed many of the selections and the executions. He saw unsuspecting prisoners selected for the gas chambers march toward their death. A few guessed what was about to happen. He remembered:

> Once a woman with four children, all holding each other by the hand to help the smallest ones over the rough ground, passed by me very slowly. She stepped very close and whispered, pointing to her four children, "How can you murder these beautiful, darling children? Don't you have any heart?"[14]

But he did not stop this or any other execution, although, he wrote, he struggled with the responsibility of killing so many people:

> I had to watch day and night, whether it was the dragging and the burning of the bodies, the teeth being ripped out, the cutting of the hair. . . . For hours I had to stand in the horrible, haunting stench while the mass graves were dug. . . . I had to do all of this because I was the one to whom everyone looked.[15]

Ich erkläre hiermit an Eidesstatt,
daß in den Jahren 1941 bis 1943
während meiner Amtszeit als KdT
des K. L. Auschwitz 2 Millionen
Juden durch Vergasung und ca.
1/2 Million auf andere Weise zu Tode
gebracht worden.

Nbg. 14. 5. 1946   Rudolf Höß

The above was written & signed before me
at Nuremberg, Germany on May 14, 1946.

Josef Maier
Chief, Analysis Section
Interrogations Division
Office of U.S. Chief of Counsel

Rudolph Höss observed many of the executions in the gas chambers at Auschwitz. This affadavit was signed by Höss on May 14, 1946, stating that "2 million Jews were put to death by gassing and 1/2 million by other means" during his time as commandant.

What kind of person was he? In the end, he believed that he was "gentle, good-natured, and very helpful, [but] I became the greatest destroyer of human beings . . . a blind, obedient robot who carried out every order."[16]

A Final Execution

After the war, Rudolf Höss went into hiding. Auschwitz survivors reported the crimes that he and his guards had committed. British authorities were especially keen to capture him. Knowing that he was most likely alone and hard to find, they concentrated instead on locating his wife and children.

Rudolph Höss (center, bareheaded) just before his execution in Auschwitz on April 16, 1947.

On March 6, 1946, nine months after the war ended, his wife was arrested and placed in a German prison. Officials interrogated her about the whereabouts of her husband. She would only tell them that Rudolf Höss was dead. Instead, the officers decided to trick her.

They arranged for a train to be placed on a track that ran directly behind Mrs. Höss's prison cell. As one of the British officers recalled, they informed Mrs. Höss that the train would

take her three sons to Siberia unless she told us where her husband was. . . . If she did not do this then she would have two minutes to say goodbye to her sons. . . . We left her for ten minutes . . . to write down the information we required. Fortunately our bluff worked; she wrote down the information and she and her sons were sent home.[17]

The next day, using the information that his wife had provided, authorities arrested Rudolf Höss. A year later, his trial took less than three weeks. At the end, he was sentenced to death. On April 16, 1947, he was hanged at Auschwitz I on a gallows erected directly behind the first gas chamber.

3 Pery Broad

A staunch Nazi from childhood, Pery Broad volunteered to be a member of the SS and was sent to be a guard at Auschwitz in 1942. Then he was transferred to the political division of Auschwitz, which conducted brutal interrogations as well as executions of certain prisoners. In this job, Broad witnessed—but seemed not to participate in—many horrific episodes.

This is the Black Wall between Blocks 10 and 11. SS camp guard Pery Broad witnessed many executions at the Black Wall.

The Black Wall of Block 11

At first, Broad was assigned to the camp jail, Block 11, where prisoners were tortured and killed, especially in the early days of the camp. According to Broad, prisoners who had committed a crime, even a small infraction, were often taken to Block 11 and given a sentence: penal code 1 or 2. Those who received the first would receive a beating or hard labor. Those with the second sentence were executed.

The condemned prisoners were taken to a nearby washroom where they were told to undress. Broad described it in an account that he wrote when he was arrested after the war:

> The victims seemed already to know that in a few minutes they would be freed from their tortures and their sufferings. The helpers wrote the prisoner's numbers with indelible pencils on the naked bodies of the victims, to make the identification of the bodies in the mortuary or in the crematorium possible.[1]

Then the condemned prisoners were taken outside to the courtyard between Blocks 11 and 10, with high walls and barricaded windows. These early executions were carried out with a small-caliber pistol, so as not to create much noise. Broad described the executions in this way:

> *A prisoner would stand near the black wall with a spade in his hand. Another prisoner belonging to the cleaning squad and specially chosen for his strength approached at a run, quickly pushing the first two victims forward. He kept a fast hold on their arms and then pressed their faces to the wall. . . . Some of those walking skeletons had spent months in the stinking cells, where not even animals would be kept, and they could barely manage to stand straight. And yet, at that last moment, many of them shouted, "Long live Poland," or "Long live freedom." The executioner was then in a particular hurry to shoot them.*[2]

Witness to the Gassing

Broad was a witness when the first transport of Jews arrived from Upper Silesia (part of Poland) on February 15, 1942. They would be sent to Crematorium I, originally a storage area of turnips and other vegetables. There they would become the first transport of Jews to be gassed at Auschwitz.[3]

To keep the planned executions as secret as possible, streets near the crematorium were blocked, and all offices that faced it were closed as the Jews left the train.

A man playing an accordion leads a sing-along with a group of SS officers at their retreat at Solahuette outside Auschwitz in July 1944. Despite the horrific murders that the SS camp guards and officers committed every day, they maintained a regular life outside of the camp. Pery Broad served in the SS at Auschwitz for about three years.

SS officers standing on the roof of the crematorium told the Jews that, once they had showered, they would be taken to their new barracks and given hot soup. They were told to place their shoes next to their clothing when they undressed so that they would be easy to find afterward. Then they went inside the crematorium where the gas would be administered:

Everything was extremely tidy. But the special smell made some of them uneasy. They looked in vain for the showers or water pipes fixed to the ceiling. The hall meanwhile was getting packed. . . . As soon as the last person had entered . . . the door was closed. . . . Those inside heard the heavy bolts secured. . . . A deadly, paralyzing terror spread among the victims. They started to beat upon the door. . . . Derisive laughter was the only reply. Somebody shouted through the door, "Don't get burnt, while you take your bath!" Several victims noticed that covers had been removed from the six holes in the ceiling. They uttered a loud cry of terror when they saw a head in a gas-mask at one opening.[4]

Then the canisters containing Zyklon B were opened, and the blue crystals "the size of peas" were dropped through the vents into the crematorium below.[5] At the same time, an SS officer signaled a nearby truck to gun its engine to mask the cries of the people inside the crematorium.

In less than five minutes, Broad remembered, the terrible cries had ended.

ZYKLON B

A canister and pellets of Zyklon B. This poison was first used at Auschwitz to kill lice and prevent the spread of typhus.

From the time that the first prisoners arrived, Auschwitz was a filthy camp where lice thrived. To prevent typhus, which is spread by lice, SS camp officials used an insecticide, Zyklon B, to clean prisoners' clothing and barracks.[6] In order to do this, the building had to be sealed, fumigated, and then aired out for twenty-four hours.

Sometimes buildings were treated for much less time. One Soviet prisoner, Andrey Pogozhev, recalled that he and other POWs were taken to the bathhouse while their barrack was fumigated. Allowed to return after only three hours, they entered their room while the smell of Zyklon B still filled the air. The odor made the prisoners so sick that they began to vomit, but guards forced them to stay in the room all night. By morning, a third of men in the room "lay motionless with blue lips and blackened faces. Most of them died without coming to their senses."[7]

An SS officer who saw how the powerful insecticide worked drew a conclusion: "If Zyklon B could be used to kill lice, why could it not be used to kill human pests?"[8] After a few experiments to kill prisoners in the basement of Block 11, Zyklon B revealed how effective it could be at killing people. If the room temperature was at least 80.6 degrees Fahrenheit, the crystals vaporized into a lethal gas that could kill a chamber of people in only a few minutes. The crystals were also a cheap method of execution: less than nine pounds of the crystals were necessary to kill about one thousand people.[9]

Pery Broad witnessed the construction of Birkenau. This is the unloading ramp and the main gate called the "Gate of Death" at Auschwitz-Birkenau.

Building Birkenau

For the duration of the war, Pery Broad stayed at Auschwitz, observing everything that happened.

He was there when the sub-camp at Auschwitz-Birkenau was built. Conditions there were much worse than at Auschwitz I. He remembered:

> Feet sank into a sticky bog at every step. There was hardly any water for washing. The prisoners slept, six to a bed, on wooden planks placed in three tiers. Most of the beds were without straw pallets. The roll-call held twice daily meant standing for hours in wet and cold weather with mire underfoot. If it rained in the daytime, the prisoners would be obliged to lie on the beds in their wet clothes. No wonder that several hundred of them died every day.[10]

He was an observer when the Soviet POWs, who had helped to build the camp, were finally executed:

> Thousands of POWs were shot in a wood near Birkenau and were buried in large collective graves, one layer of corpses lying on another. The graves were some 50 to 60 metres long, 4 metres deep and their width was probably 4 metres too. The camp authorities had thus solved the Russian problem to their utmost satisfaction.[11]

Time after time, he witnessed all of the atrocities, including the events of the final days as Auschwitz was evacuated. The Germans tried to burn as many documents as possible. "In front of the administration buildings . . . piles of personal documents were set on fire and those buildings, in which the greatest mass murders had been committed . . . were blown up."[12]

After the War

After the war, authorities detained Broad. During this time, in July 1945, possibly to win some favor, he wrote an account of the SS crimes at Auschwitz. He described the crimes of others and included himself only as an observer. After a while, he was released and worked in business. In 1959, he was again arrested as German officials began a more detailed investigation of the atrocities at Auschwitz.

During this trial, witnesses to Pery Broad's crimes testified against him. His defense maintained that he simply observed—and did not participate in—them. Witnesses disagreed. One witness, his former clerk, recalled that, after joking about victims "spurting" blood during an execution against the Black Wall, he handed his coat to his clerk for cleaning. The clerk told the court that "[i]t was spattered with fresh blood." When Broad was asked about the clerk's testimony, Broad said, "I always stood so far from the Black Wall that I could not be spattered."[13]

His former clerk also testified about Pery Broad's experiences at Auschwitz II:

> [O]nce a boy of ten to twelve was brought to Broad's office. The child had arrived in Auschwitz on a transport of Hungarians and apparently had been able to escape selection by hiding. Amid tears the boy assured Broad, displaying his childlike hands, that he was strong and able to work. Broad just laughed, told the guard who had escorted the boy to take him to the others, and pointed in the direction of the gas chamber.[14]

At the end of the trial, which lasted from December 1963 until August 1965, Broad was sentenced to four years in prison. When he was released, he was again able to go on with his life and continue his employment in business.[15]

On October 7, 1941, Andrey Pogozhev arrived in Auschwitz. Captured by German troops, Andrey was one of ten thousand Soviet POWs sent to Auschwitz to help build Auschwitz-Birkenau.

Upon arrival, he and his fellow prisoners were confronted by armed SS guards and a prisoner kommando of barbers. The POWs had no idea where they were, but one of the barbers told them they had arrived at the "terrible camp" of Auschwitz.[1]

The First Death

Next they were told to undress and leave everything they had so that they could be disinfected.

A fellow prisoner who was a proud father tried to keep a cherished photograph of his young daughter. Outside, near the

A large group of Soviet POWs arrive at Auschwitz. Andrey Pogozhev was one of the ten thousand Soviet POWs sent to Auschwitz to help build Birkenau.

disinfection tank, an SS guard saw him with the photo and knocked it out of his hand with his whip. Andrey saw that the prisoner then "bent down to pick up the photo but a lash of the whip got him upright straight away. The [SS guard] stepped forward and with unhidden spite trod on the photo, then smeared it in the mud."[2]

Angered by the guard's cruelty, the Soviet prisoner hit the guard, nearly knocking him into the disinfectant tank. Then a nearby SS officer pulled out his pistol and shot the man to death. That was Andrey's introduction to life at KL-Auschwitz.

Transformed into Animals

Andrey could not believe what he experienced at the beginning of his stay. Not given any clothing after their disinfection, the POWs had only a cotton blanket and a tin for soup.

Our first days in Auschwitz dumbfounded us. They transformed us from human beings into a herd of animals. . . . Everyone had to be present for roll-call. Sick men . . . even dead men . . . would be brought out from the blocks. Roll-call lasted for two hours. Consequently, columns of naked Soviet POWs would stagger into line and stand the whole time, the sick and the dead stretched out on the concrete in front of them.[3]

For almost two months, they lived this way. Finally, in late November, they were taken to the shower room for the first time since they had arrived.

> When we refused to wash in the freezing water they turned the fire hoses on us, blasting us with icy jets from high pressure nozzles. Aiming at our eyes, ears, mouths, and bellies, the cold water cut, choked, burned and blinded. Those caught by the blasts . . . fell, seeking salvation under benches and behind the bodies of those who'd dropped unconscious.[4]

After this ordeal, they were given clothes that had clearly belonged to other Soviet POWs who had been executed sometime earlier.

Building Birkenau

In January 1942, Andrey and the other Soviet POWs were marched to Birkenau each morning to help build the newly planned camp. Starving, but forced to work more than ever, the prisoners craved food, no matter what the consequences were.

Andrey remembered what happened during February 1942. One morning, the POWs passed by a mound of beets, intended for the camp kitchens, by the side of the road. That evening after work, on their way back to Auschwitz I, the men were unable to control themselves. Dozens of prisoners swooped down on the pile, trying to grab a beet. The lucky ones then tried to hide their prize and blend back into the line of prisoners. But the SS guards began to shoot the hungry looters still looking for food:

> *The whole drama was over in a few minutes but left us deep in shock. The march back to camp continued in silence. On reaching the gates . . . the officer of the day . . . began running along our column with his whip, beating heads and jabbing faces.*[5]

The next month, they were moved to Birkenau. By then, of the 10,000 Soviet POWs once taken to Auschwitz, only 666 remained.[6] Now that they were out of the compact and well-guarded camp of Auschwitz I, Andrey saw some hope that he might be able to escape from the vast camp at Birkenau.

Prisoners at work building Crematorium IV at Auschwitz-Birkenau.

A Stay in the Hospital

At Birkenau, Andrey was one of twenty-five men assigned to the housekeeping kommando. Their duties included collecting the bodies of prisoners who had died during the night, removing their clothing, and sending them to the crematorium.

On March 30, 1942, Andrey spent the better part of the day with his housekeeping kommando, removing corpses and helping other prisoners who were barely alive. Afterward, he stepped outside one barrack in order to clean his hands before eating his evening ration of food. A ditch of water ran along a barbed-wire fence; he and his kommando members had often used that ditch for washing. As he stooped down to rinse his hands, a guard shot him through the hand.

He was taken to the hospital in Auschwitz I and allowed to remain there some three months until his wound had healed. When he returned to Birkenau at the end of June, only 150 Soviet POWs were alive.[7]

Planning the Escape

Around this time Andrey and six other Soviet POWs began to plan an escape. They decided that it should occur while they were on search duty. Whenever a prisoner went missing at evening roll call, prisoners in the search kommando went outside the camp to look for the prisoner.

Although Soviet POWs had never been selected for search duty, they decided to change that. Andrey and the others talked to the Block Leader of their barracks, trying to convince him that the Russians would do a better job searching for any missing prisoners. After ten days, they were given the chance to begin search duty.

These are pages from the Auschwitz camp hospital register. Red crosses in the last columns indicate the death of patients. Andrey was taken to the camp hospital in Auschwitz I after a guard shot him in the hand.

Working on the search kommando allowed the committee to find the best place to make an escape. Then they selected the date for the escape: November 6, 1942. To make certain that search duty would be necessary that day, they planned to bury the body of a dead prisoner outside the camp; he would become the missing prisoner. As the day neared, they told other Soviet POWs of the plan, so that a mass escape could take place.

Escaping the Camp

At evening roll call on the appointed day, the search kommando marched outside the camp. As the prisoners pretended to search for the missing man, a guard dog discovered the hidden body, something that the planners had not anticipated. SS guards ordered Andrey and three other men to recover the body. Andrey was worried; he wanted to run and not return the body to the camp.

At that very moment, Soviet prisoners inside the camp stormed the closest guard tower, pushing it over and knocking down the electrified barbed-wire fence. As they escaped into the darkness of the surrounding forest, Andrey and the search kommando fled as well. In all, some seventy Soviet prisoners attempted to flee that night. Most were captured or killed, but Andrey and at least two others made it past the German searchers.

Eventually, he was able to make his way back to the Soviet Union where he was reunited with his family. He was one of the few Soviet POWs to survive Auschwitz.

Identifying the Guilty

In 1965, Andrey was a witness at a trial in Frankfurt-am-Main, Germany, for war crimes committed at Auschwitz. He recalled:

> *For many years I'd been trying to forget the most terrible things. I'd been trying to preserve only the good and dear recollections from that terrible time. . . . Did I imagine that one day I'd have to remember . . . the tragedy of my days in Hell? . . . Of course not! But I had to remember.*[8]

Seated in the courtroom, Andrey was asked to identify the accused who were alleged to have committed war crimes there.

Andrey was nervous and confused. Twenty years had gone by since the war; the accused men were older and looked quite different now. "Dressed in brand-new suits, clean-shaven with well-groomed faces, sleek hair perfectly parted, they stood like gentlemen who'd accidentally strayed into the hall from a banquet," Andrey recalled in a book that he wrote after the war.[9]

Andrey took his time in the courtroom, studying the men's faces and their mannerisms. Suddenly he was able to remember who they were. He was even able to identify the SS officer who had killed the prisoner on Andrey's first day in Auschwitz. Andrey asked himself:

Andrey Pogozhev was able to identify the SS officer, Hans Stark (pictured here), who murdered his comrade when Andrey first arrived at Auschwitz. Stark received a ten-year prison sentence for his war crimes.

> *Was it you who murdered my comrade . . . over a photograph of his daughter? The little girl whose photo your [SS guard] trampled in the mud? . . . His eyelid trembled. I guessed he'd recognized me and his nerve was failing. . . . And despite all I endured, I remember you. I even recall the colour of your eyes. You feel nervous, don't you?*[10]

Then he pronounced the man's name aloud in the courtroom, "Hans Stark." Thanks in part to Pogozhev's testimony, Stark was sentenced to ten years in prison.[11]

5 Walter Winter

A member of the Roma community, Walter Winter knew at an early age that he was different from most Germans:

> [E]ven as children we were discriminated against. When as a child you had barely learnt to walk and started to play with other children, adults or even children themselves called out, "Gypsy! Gypsy!" At that age children do not know what they are saying. This insult had been learnt in the parental home from the parents.[1]

He and his family were not about to let that prejudice stand in their way. Even when Germany enacted anti-Roma measures, his father told the family to speak only German—never the Romani language—and keep a low profile. Still, they could not change their appearance. As Walter recalled, his family "was dressed no differently from others, but we were dark skinned. . . . In those days there were very few people of dark appearance [in Germany]. When people saw a person of dark appearance they immediately saw a Gypsy."[2]

Despite this prejudice, in January 1940, Walter was drafted into the German navy, where he served for two years. Although others were promoted, he was overlooked because he was considered "non-Aryan" (that is a "genetically inferior non-German"). He was discharged as "unsuitable material" and returned home.[3]

WALTER WINTER, PART OF THE ROMA AND SINTI

A Roma woman with her children in Poland. The Roma and Sinti faced brutal persecution from the Nazis.

To the Germans, Walter Winter was a "Gypsy," or *zigeuner*—derogatory words in either language. But Walter identified himself as a member of the Roma and, more specifically, as a member of the Sinti. That is, if the Roma people could be compared to Americans, the Sinti would be New Yorkers, or a subgroup of the whole.

The Roma migrated to southeastern Europe in the 1200s. Because people thought they had come from Egypt, they were called "Gypsies." In fact, they had actually migrated from northern India.

Because they had darker skin than most Europeans, they were considered "evil" by medieval Christians. Myths about Gypsies were perpetuated: They were said to steal and eat babies; they were also accused of making "the nails with which Jesus was crucified."[4] For these reasons, the Roma were discriminated against; they were either used as forced laborers or run out of town. Many laws were enacted in Europe that discriminated against the Roma.

A year later, in March 1943, he and his brother, Erich, were arrested and transported to Auschwitz, along with approximately 23,000 other Roma and Sinti.[5]

Life and Death in the "Gypsy Camp"

From the moment that he arrived in Auschwitz on March 14, 1943, Walter realized how terrible his life was about to become. As the Roma prisoners were marched from the train station to the main camp, they passed a line of workers.

> They were carrying two corpses covered in blood. The corpses were slung from poles, tied by the hands and feet, like deer. Two men carried each corpse, streaming with blood. . . . Having seen this we were so demoralized that we were unable to mutter a word.[6]

Tattooed with a number that began with Z (for "zigeuner"), he and his brother were sent with the other Roma to the "Gypsy Camp" in Auschwitz II, where entire families were allowed to stay together.

Since they had both served in the German armed services before their arrest, Erich and Walter were given administrative jobs. Erich was block senior, charged with keeping the barracks clean; Walter was the block roll-call clerk; his job was to keep accurate records and record all deaths.

This is one of the few remaining photos from the "Gypsy Camp." Like all Roma and Sinti prisoners, this woman was given a number beginning with the letter "Z" for "zigeuner." Her name is unknown, but she arrived at the camp on October 10, 1943.

Their barrack was so overcrowded that between 700 and 800 Roma lived in their block—about 500 too many.[7] Children, especially, were affected by the overcrowding and often died of disease. Walter had to take their bodies from the bunks and place them outside the block on the ground. Then he had to fill out death certificates for each corpse. They also lived closest of all the barracks to Crematorium III. Walter and the other Roma smelled the odor of burning bodies daily.

The Roma were not safe in the Gypsy Camp, especially if they came down with disease. Only a week after Walter arrived, 1,700 Roma were gassed when their block came down with typhus. They were taken by truck directly to the gas chamber and killed. In May, another block of 1,035 Roma were gassed when they came down with typhoid.[8]

Walter and men in his barracks planned to fight back if the SS ever came to transport his block to the gas chamber, but they never did.

The Boots of Hungarian Jews

Once full of 23,000 Roma, the Gypsy Camp eventually dwindled in size, as selections for the gas chamber and disease had reduced the number of people living there.

Beginning in May 1944, trainloads of Hungarian Jews arrived at Auschwitz II. One night, a train awakened Walter:

> The way to crematorium 3 led past the Gypsy Camp. There were bunkers with SS guards en route. This particular night the people found out that they were destined for the crematorium. They resisted and the SS mowed down the entire column. Every single person. Everyone on the road was shot dead.[9]

Because there were so many Hungarian Jews, not all could be gassed immediately. Sometimes, the SS selected men from the transports and placed them in a section of the Gypsy Camp.

Walter noticed two things about the Jewish men who shared the Roma camp: They had "beautiful laced boots" and they were not required to work.[10] Each morning, he watched as one or two blocks were led out of the camp to the gas chamber. Around the

A large pile of shoes found at Auschwitz after it was liberated. Boots and shoes were important to camp prisoners in order to survive the cold weather. Walter Winter gave up his bread ration to trade for a pair of boots.

same time, he noticed that some Roma men began to wear the same boots, instead of their usual clogs. Walter realized that they had bartered part of their daily bread ration for the boots. He decided to do the same.

He approached a man standing next to his teenage son and offered bread for the man's boots. At first the man refused even though he was hungry. Finally, Walter said:

> "Here, take this piece of bread. I'll bring you this evening's ration too if you give me your boots. I'll also give you the shoes I'm wearing. You don't need to go barefoot." He agreed and I took the boots. Next day they were gassed.[11]

The End of the Gypsy Camp

By May 1944, only 6,000 Roma were left in the Gypsy Camp. At that point, the camp commanders decided to put an end to the camp. On May 25, they selected 1,500 Roma to be transferred to other concentration camps.[12] On August 2, the camp was told that there would be a transport to a better place for the Roma. The transport would include all former members of the German armed forces and their families.

Everyone in the transport, including Walter and his brother, Erich, was placed in train cars and taken away. The 2,897 remaining Roma in the Gypsy Camp were told that they would follow soon.[13] Most of them were older men, women, and children. Instead, on the night of August 2, 1944, the camp was surrounded by SS guards. In half-hour intervals, the Roma were taken to Crematoria II and V to be gassed. By August 3, the entire camp was empty.

Of the 23,000 Roma sent to Auschwitz, 20,000 died there.[14]

Safe at Last

Walter was fortunate because he was on the last Roma transport out of Auschwitz. His luck lasted until he saw where he had been taken: Ravensbrück, another concentration camp. Walter was transferred to one concentration camp, then another. He suffered through brutal forced labor and horrible conditions until near the end of the war.

As the war came to a close, he was drafted back into the German army to fight the Soviets. He and his brother were given

A group of Romani prisoners sit on the ground awaiting directions from the Nazi guards at the Belzec concentration camp in 1940. Belzec would later become a death camp. It is unknown the exact number of Roma killed during the Holocaust, but about twenty thousand were killed at Auschwitz.

uniforms, but no helmets or weapons. Of four thousand or so Roma who were drafted to fight the Russians at the end of the war, only seven hundred survived.[15] Although he was wounded, Walter survived along with his brother; they were reunited with their parents.

Long after the war, in 1986, he and his wife went on a vacation to a beach resort far from Germany. While there, a German man befriended them. One day, the man asked Walter about his Z tattoo. Walter told him that he had been in a concentration camp. Then the man said that he had been in the SS, though in a part unrelated to the concentration camps. Walter let the man talk, but he immediately felt a great hostility toward him. When the man invited Walter and his wife to visit at his home in Germany, Walter believed that he was simply trying to ease his guilty conscience.

At the end of a book about his experience as a Roma in Germany before and during World War II, Walter wrote:

> *In books you read: [Auschwitz] was like this, and this. The authors always write that so and so many people were murdered and that the people were maltreated. That is correct, that is all true, but you don't read about the feelings, the constant fear. There are things that people cannot begin to comprehend. Yet I remember everything. . . . We in the camps were forced to accept everything; we were completely powerless. Then this humiliation because of your so-called "racial origin." Is this my fault? Is this the fault of my parents? And that is what I fear, that these right-wing extremists, these Nazis, will get the upper hand once again.[16]*

6   Dr. Miklos Nyiszli

s World War II began, Dr. Miklos Nyiszli, like other
Hungarian Jews, was in a dangerous position. Between
1938 and 1941, as an ally of Germany, Hungary
enacted a series of racial laws, which removed the citizenship
rights that Jews had held in Hungary since 1867.[1] Many things
were forbidden, such as marriage to non-Jews and employment in
certain professions, including the armed services. Eventually, Jews
were forced to work under terrible conditions on construction
projects related to the war. Still, Hungarian authorities refused
to deport Jews to German concentration camps.

As the war continued, Hitler was not satisfied with Hungary's
refusal to implement the "final solution to the Jewish Question."
On March 19, 1944, following rumors that Hungary might seek a
separate peace with the West, German troops occupied Hungary.
As a result, all Jews were placed under house arrest and their
property confiscated. They were forced into ghettos, before
being placed on cattle cars, and shipped mostly to Auschwitz.
Dr. Nyiszli and his family were part of the first deportations.

A Special Selection

When they arrived at the camp, Nyiszli, his wife, and his
fourteen-year-old daughter were selected for the able-bodied line

of arrivals. Then the medical doctor in charge of the Auschwitz selection process, Josef Mengele, asked all doctors to step out of line. Not knowing what to expect, some fifty doctors moved forward, among them Dr. Nyiszli. Next, Dr. Mengele asked if any of the doctors had studied in Germany and were acquainted with pathology and forensic medicine. Only Dr. Nyiszli stepped forward. That step secured him a place as Dr. Mengele's personal research pathologist and a residence in a crematorium where the Sonderkommando lived. He would not see his wife and daughter again until after the war.

A group of Jewish men stand in line after being selected and processed for forced labor at Auschwitz in May 1944. Dr. Miklos Nyiszli, his wife, and his daughter were selected for work when they arrived at Auschwitz.

The Results of the Gas Chamber

In his work for Dr. Mengele, Nyiszli had to observe the procedure at the gas chamber and crematorium. The first time that he witnessed the gassings was just after his arrival at Auschwitz II. A whistle one evening signaled that a transport train had arrived. From his window in one crematorium he saw Jewish prisoners forced from the cars. At the same time, he heard the Sonderkommando prepare the furnace for the cremations.

After this trainload of people was killed, Nyiszli visited the gas chamber where their bodies lay. He remembered:

The bodies were not lying here and there throughout the room, but piled in a mass to the ceiling. The reason for this was that the gas first inundated the lower layers of air and rose but slowly towards the ceiling. . . . I noticed that the bodies of the women, the children, and the aged were at the bottom of the pile; at the top, the strongest. . . . Blood oozed from their noses and mouths; their faces, bloated and blue, were so deformed as to be almost unrecognizable. Nevertheless some of the Sonderkommando often did recognize their kin. . . . I had no reason to be here, and yet I had come down among the dead.

> *I felt it my duty to my people and to the entire world to be able to give an accurate account of what I had seen if ever, by some miraculous whim of fate, I should escape.*[2]

Doing His Job

One day members of the Sonderkommando called Nyiszli into the gas chamber. In the twisted pile of bodies left there after a gassing, they had found a teenaged girl who was still alive:

> *We removed the still-living body from the corpses pressing against it. . . . I took out my syringe and . . . administered three intravenous injections. My companions covered her body which was as cold as ice with a heavy overcoat. One ran to the kitchen to fetch some tea and warm broth. Everybody wanted to help, as if she were his own child.*[3]

When the teenaged girl had recovered, Nyiszli and the members of the Sonderkommando tried to find a way to save her life. They thought about sending her to join a woman's work camp, but she looked too young. They also worried that the girl would want to tell someone what had happened; telling her story

PLUNDERING THE DEAD

Bales of human hair found in one of the Auschwitz warehouses after liberation of the camp. The hair was used to make felt, thread, socks, and other cloth for the German army.

By living with the Sonderkommando, Dr. Nyiszli learned many secrets about Auschwitz, including the plunder of the victims.

As soon as the gassing was completed, dentists and others working for the Sonderkommando inspected the corpses and removed any gold crowns or fillings. Then, according to Dr. Nyiszli, the gold was placed "in buckets filled with an acid which burned off all pieces of bone and flesh. . . . I would judge that from 18 to 20 pounds of it were collected daily in each crematorium."[4]

At first, the collected gold was used for the dental work of German SS soldiers and their families. But so much was harvested from the victims in such a short time that, beginning in November 1942, the SS sent the gold to the central German bank. But not all gold left Auschwitz, since SS personnel used the looted gold for their personal gain. Some prisoners also stole it from victims and used it to buy food and other goods.[5]

Hair was also collected from people who passed the selection and people who were gassed. The hair was then bagged and sent for use in textile factories to be turned into felt, thread, and socks for submarine crews and railroad workers. When the Soviet army liberated the camp in 1945, soldiers discovered almost seven tons of human hair in 305 sacks from about 140,000 victims.[6]

Dr. Josef Mengele

would bring about the death of everyone involved. Nyiszli turned to SS sergeant Mussfeld, who was in charge of the crematoria Sonderkommando, and asked if the young girl's life could be spared.

For a few moments, Mussfeld considered the options, then said it would not be possible. "Half an hour later the young girl was led, or rather carried, into the furnace room hallways, and there Mussfeld sent another in his place to do his job. A bullet in the back of the neck."[7]

Dissecting the Dead

As a doctor, Nyiszli was assigned to care for the German guards in charge of the crematoria and the almost nine hundred prisoners of the Sonderkommando. But his most important duty, as far as Dr. Mengele was concerned, was the dissection of the dead.

Given an examination room near one of the crematoria in Auschwitz II, Dr. Nyiszli dissected any bodies that Dr. Mengele sent to him and wrote careful autopsy reports about his findings. An expert pathologist, Dr. Nyiszli was shocked to find that many of the autopsies were to be performed on twins, because Mengele conducted perverse experiments on them. What he quickly discovered was that the twins did not die from natural causes; they had been injected with chloroform directly into their hearts.

Some of the autopsies he performed were on disabled individuals, selected purposefully by Dr. Mengele. One day, while reviewing a trainload of new arrivals for selection, Dr. Mengele spied a man with his teenage son. Of particular interest to Mengele was the fact that the father had a hunched back while the son had a deformed foot. Since Mengele wanted to prove that Jews were genetically inferior, he selected them for a special examination by Dr. Nyiszli. During the exam, the man told Nyiszli that they had spent almost five horrific years in the ghetto at Litzmannstadt (the German name for Lodz, Poland) until the Germans deported them to Auschwitz.

Nyiszli understood the terrible dilemma he faced:

I, a Jewish doctor, had to examine them with exact clinical methods before they died, and then perform the dissection on their still warm bodies. So shaken was I by the situation, about which I was powerless to do anything at all, that I suddenly felt myself spinning on the edge of madness. . . . Could this be the will of God? No; I could not believe it.[8]

Nyiszli offered the father and son some food. Then four members of the Sonderkommando escorted the two into the furnace room where they were ordered to undress. SS sergeant Mussfield shot them to death with his revolver.

Eva (left) and Moritz Zelmonovits, sister and brother who survived the experiments Josef Mengele performed on twins, pose for a photo in their hometown in Hungary after the war. Dr. Nyiszli witnessed Mengele's horrible experiments.

Afterward, Nyiszli was ordered to dissect the two. When he had done so, Dr. Mengele arrived to view the results. He was so taken by the cases that he told Nyiszli to cook the bodies so that the skin and organs would be removed and only their skeletons would remain. Then the skeletons were sent to the Anthropological Museum in Berlin, marked "Urgent: National Defense." Mengele was pleased that the father and son exhibited such problematic conditions, which he took to mean that Jews were a degenerate people. Nyiszli, however, noted in his book that their abnormalities were "common to hundreds of thousands of men of all races

A written request for the pathological examination of a twelve-year-old boy's head in the Birkenau camp hospital, signed in the lower right corner by Josef Mengele. Dr. Nyiszli had to perform such pathology exams during his time at Auschwitz.

Hyg.-bakt. Unters.-Stelle
der Waffen-SS, Südost

29. JUN. 1944

Auschwitz OS., am **29. Juni 1944.**

Anliegend wird übersandt:

(12-jähriges Kind)

Material: **Kopf einer Leiche** entnommen am

zu untersuchen auf **Histologische Schnitte**

Name, Vorname:

Dienstgrad, Einheit: **siehe Anlage**

Klinische Diagnose:

Anschrift der einsendenden Dienststelle: **H.-Krankenbau**
Zigeunerlager Auschwitz II, B II e

Bemerkungen:

Der 1. Lagerarzt
K.L. Auschwitz II

SS-Hauptsturmführer.
(Stempel, Unterschrift)

and climates."[9] The Nazis' claim that Jews and others were genetically inferior to "Aryans" was completely false.

After the War

Nyiszli continued his work for Dr. Mengele until the doctor vanished one day and was replaced by someone new. Not long after that, in the early morning hours of January 18, 1945, Nyiszli heard machine guns and small explosions. The SS was evacuating the camp before the Soviet army arrived. Nyiszli survived a forced march, or "death march," and more than three months in various other prison camps.

After the war he returned home, sick at heart at what he had experienced. Then one day, a few weeks later, the doorbell rang. His wife and his daughter had survived the war. They had been transferred from Auschwitz to the Bergen-Belsen concentration camp. They cried and held each other. Before he died of a heart attack in 1956, Nyiszli wrote about his experiences at Auschwitz, including the reunion with his family:

I knew it would take much time and infinite patience before we could resume any sort of really normal life. But all that mattered was that we were alive . . . and together again. Life suddenly became meaningful again. I would begin practicing, yes. . . . But I swore as long as I lived I would never lift a scalpel again.[10]

7   Shlomo Dragon

oon after the German army invaded Poland on September 1, 1939, seventeen-year-old Shlomo Dragon and his twenty-year-old brother, Abraham, were identified as Jews and forced to harvest potatoes near their town of Zuromin. One day, after a few weeks of forced labor, they returned from the fields to find that all of the Jews in their town had been sent to Warsaw. After the potato harvest was over, they, too, were sent to Warsaw, where a Jewish ghetto was soon established by the Nazis.

For the next three years, the brothers relied on their wits to escape the ghetto and avoid being sent to a forced labor camp. During that time, their father died of starvation and their oldest sister died of illness in the Warsaw ghetto. They also learned that their mother, younger sister, and younger brother were transported to a labor camp; what they did not know until much later was that they had then been shipped to Auschwitz where they were all killed.

In late fall 1942, the brothers' luck ran out. Arrested and jailed for a short time, the brothers were placed in a cattle car with so many people that no one could sit down or move. They rode for two days. They had no idea what awaited them when the train stopped.

When Shlomo and Abraham were selected to work for the Sonderkommando, one of the first things they saw was a hut filled with clothes that had been taken from the prisoners. This is one of the warehouses in Auschwitz, which had clothes spilling out of it when the camp was liberated in January 1945.

Arrival in Auschwitz

On the night of December 7, 1942, Shlomo and Abraham arrived at Auschwitz. Shlomo remembered that SS guards "opened the doors and greeted us straightaway with beatings. . . . Left behind in the cars were old people and children who had been crushed or had died for some reason. During the trip . . . we had had nothing to drink."[1]

When the selection took place, Shlomo and Abraham were chosen for the able-bodied line of prisoners. Then they were told that they had been picked for work in a factory.

They were tattooed and were sent to a barrack in Birkenau. Only then did they learn that they had been selected to work in the Sonderkommando.

Selected for the Sonderkommando

The next day they were taken to a hut next to the "little white house" or Bunker 2, where larger groups of victims were gassed. The SS officer opened the hut door revealing piles of clothing from men, women, and children. "They were lying there as if the people who'd worn them had just undressed," Shlomo explained in an interview after the war.[2]

Divided into two teams of workers, one group, which included Abraham, stayed in the hut bundling the discarded clothing. Shlomo was with the other group, as it was led to Bunker 2. Then the SS commander opened the bunker door and Shlomo saw that

. . . bodies fell out. We smelled gas. We saw corpses. . . . The dead bodies were lying there, closely packed together, on top of each other, so that when the door opened they all fell and piled up next to the door. . . . Almost all of us went into shock. We stared at each other without uttering a sound. . . . We'd never seen anything like it before.[3]

That day, Shlomo dragged the bodies to carts so that they could be transported to the burning pit outside.

Both brothers quickly learned that their kommando of perhaps two hundred prisoners was divided into different work groups. Some gathered clothes, others sorted personal items, while others removed the gold from the victims' mouths, and collected their hair and glasses. Still others carted the bodies to one of the four nearby open pits, where another team threw the bodies into the pit to be burned by the SS. Other Sonderkommando members even had to crush the bones that remained after cremation and then dispose of the ashes. It was no wonder that the Germans eventually referred to them as "bearers of secrets" and attempted to make certain that none would survive to tell their story.[4]

When permanent work assignments were made, the two brothers were given barrack room duty. They only had to help with the removal and cremation of the bodies when there were large transports. Otherwise, their duties were to clean the barrack, distribute food, and wash the dishes. Even so, when the Sonderkommando came back from the gas chambers and fire pits, they shared stories of what they had seen, so the two brothers were never spared from the horrors of the camp.

The Fear of Death

When the four large crematoria at Birkenau were built, replacing the two bunkers, the Dragon brothers lived in rooms above Crematorium IV.

The procedure for gassing the selected people from the transports was almost always the same, according to Shlomo. The victims had no idea that they were about to be killed.

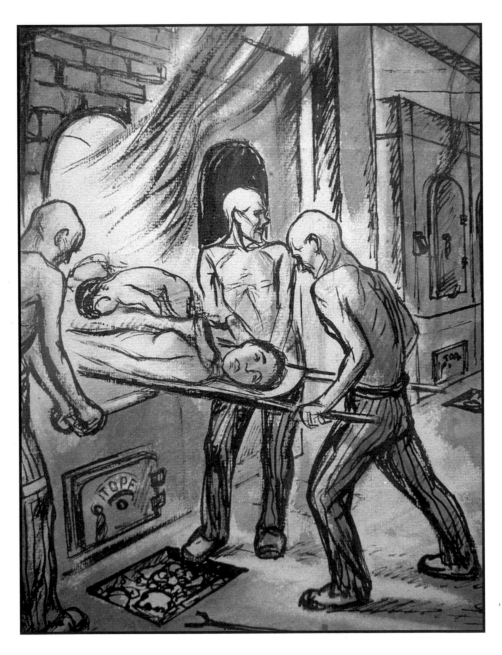

Members of the Sonderkommando insert bodies of fellow Jews into the crematory ovens in this ink drawing by David Olere, a Holocaust survivor who worked in the Sonderkommando at Auschwitz. Shlomo Dragon was forced to take on this duty sometimes during his time at the death camp.

Tired, hungry, and thirsty from their long train journey, the selected prisoners walked to the crematorium. As Shlomo described it:

> Only when they were already in the gas chamber did they sense that something was out of whack. When the gas chamber filled up, the Germans stood at the door with dogs and continued to push the people in so that more than were already inside could be gassed. Those who hadn't gone in yet began to shout. The Germans responded with murderous beatings. The people were already naked and defenseless, so they were pushed in by force. The moment the gas chamber filled up, the SS man closed the door. . . . Right after that, SS men drove over in a car that carried the emblem of the Red Cross. The cans of gas were taken out of the car and opened, and their contents were thrown into the gas chamber through the opening in the wall.[5]

The brothers lived with the fear of death, for they knew that members of the Sonderkommando were routinely selected for execution. Sometimes, entire Sonderkommando units were killed to ensure that the workers would never tell what they had seen.

A group of Jewish women and children walk toward the gas chambers after being selected for death. Shlomo Dragon witnessed the selections many times and said that the victims did not know they were about to be killed.

Whenever a Sonderkommando member was executed, he was always replaced by a new arrival from a transport.

Still, the brothers held on to the hope that they might survive Auschwitz.

The Sonderkommando Uprising

From time to time, some of the Sonderkommando thought about staging an uprising. To succeed, they knew that prisoners in Auschwitz I and II would have to join together to take control of the camp. "We wanted to carry out the uprising together with rebels in the Auschwitz I camp. . . . We wanted to blow up the camp and kill the Germans," Shlomo recalled.[6]

According to Shlomo, in late 1943, the ideas began to take shape. Shlomo was given a number of crude grenades made with gunpowder and cans. The explosive material had come from female workers at a nearby slave labor munitions factory. Shlomo hid the grenades under his mattress. He concealed others in one of the crematorium walls. He learned that he wasn't alone; prisoners at the other crematoria also were storing the homemade explosives. Shlomo did not even tell his brother, Abraham, about the grenades.

The uprising finally occurred on October 7, 1944, in the yard outside Crematorium IV. Using stones, hammers, axes, and metal poles—whatever weapons they could find—the prisoners revolted against the SS guards. Some set Crematorium IV on fire, a signal to Sonderkommando in other crematoria that the battle had begun. The Sonderkommando at Crematorium II threw their hated kapo alive into the furnace.[7] As they saw SS troops approaching the crematorium, they fled from the camp to a granary, several miles away. There, the Germans set the building on fire, burning them alive.[8]

At the end of the revolt, Crematorium IV was destroyed and three SS officers were killed. But 451 members of the Sonderkommando had been killed; only 212 remained alive.[9] Abraham had been shot in the leg and taken to the camp hospital; Shlomo was uninjured. When the SS interrogated them, they replied that they had not known about the planned uprising.

Surviving the Impossible

On January 18, 1945, the brothers were evacuated from the camp along with the remaining Sonderkommando survivors. Abraham, unable to walk and pushed in a laundry cart by a cousin, told his brother that he should try to escape the death march. That way one of them would have the possibility of survival.

One morning, Shlomo did just that:

> As I marched, I suddenly saw a path that broke away from the main road and led to a village. . . . I told my brother, "Abraham, I'm going down that path, even if I get shot. I want to escape." It was obvious to me that the Germans would shoot at me . . . but I was determined to try. . . . I swerved onto the side path and began to flee. No one shot at me at all. It was simply a miracle; I can't explain it any other way.[10]

Reunited after the war, the brothers moved to Israel where they lived together. They remained silent about their experiences in the Sonderkommando, because they felt no one could understand the terrible experience. When they did try to talk about it with others, some people grew distant. Shlomo explained:

> *They must have thought that we'd been the murderers . . . that we committed those crimes. . . . The truth is that we were forced to work for the Germans. We had no choice but to obey. We didn't spill that blood, the Germans did. We were just their playthings. . . . They forced Jews to burn the bodies of fellow Jews . . . to grind their remains into dust . . . to drag the corpses of their brethren out of the gas chambers. This is the Germans' great crime.[11]*

About 110 of the original 2,200 Sonderkommando workers survived the war.[12]

A view of the ruins of Crematorium IV at Auschwitz-Birkenau today. Crematorium IV was set on fire and destroyed during the Sonderkommando uprising on October 7, 1944.

At the start of World War II, Anna Heilman, her sister Estusia, and her parents were about to become trapped in Warsaw, Poland. After the Nazi invasion of Poland, restrictive laws were passed almost immediately. All Jews aged ten and older were forced to wear a white armband with a blue Star of David. Jews were forced to evacuate their homes within thirty minutes or suffer the severe consequences. Her father's handicraft factory was confiscated by the Germans. Ten-foot-high walls topped with barbed wire went up around their neighborhood, boxing them in and forming what became known as the Warsaw ghetto. Life inside the ghetto was horrible.

Eventually, the Germans deported the residents of the ghetto. Among the last to go in May 1943 were Anna and her family. They were transported to Majdanek, a death camp near Lublin, in German-occupied Poland. There, the daughters were separated from their parents.

Convinced that their parents had been taken to another camp, Anna and her sister volunteered to be sent to Auschwitz in September 1943, hoping to be reunited with their parents there. What the young girls did not know is that their parents had been selected for death upon arrival at Majdanek and were killed in its gas chamber.

Anna (left) and Estusia (right) sit for a photo with their older sister Sabrina (center) taken in Warsaw in 1933. Sabrina married and moved to the Soviet Union before the war began. Anna and Estusia, with their parents, were forced to live in the Warsaw ghetto after the German invasion.

Names Become Numbers

At Auschwitz, Anna and her sister were tattooed with their identification numbers (48150 and 48149, respectively) on their left forearms. They were told to wash and then were given uniforms that had once belonged to Soviet prisoners, who had been executed before Anna and her sister had arrived. As she tried to fall asleep in a crowded bunk for the first time in Auschwitz, Anna was hungry. A good portion of her food ration had been stolen. She remembered:

> Armies of lice were crawling all over me, biting me, drawing blood. I am so squashed [in the bunk] that I can't free my hand to scratch myself. I twist and turn and eventually am able to free one hand to scratch. . . . Slowly my eyes close. I see a whole golden loaf of bread. . . . I grab it with both my hands to sink my teeth into it, when the shrill of the whistle wakes me up. I close my eyes to see my treasure once more, but my dream has flitted away.[1]

One day, she and Estusia were selected with six other girls to push a garbage cart out of the camp. At first, the weak and hungry girls were unable to push the heavy cart. But when the kapo began to beat them, the girls pushed harder, and the cart moved forward. With effort, they were able to reach the gate. There an SS guard with a dog joined the kapo. They urged the dog to attack the girls.

> *Propelled by fear, we quicken our step, too terrified to look back at the dog's . . . glistening fangs. Worked into a frenzy, the dog jumps on one of the girls and buries its teeth in her. There is a terrible scream; the girl falls down. . . . I hang my head and go on. . . . A corpse is left behind on the road.*[2]

This striped skirt was part of a prison uniform worn by women at Auschwitz-Birkenau. Anna and her sister received uniforms after their arrival at Auschwitz.

Slave Laborers at the Munitions Factory

Hoping to avoid such heavy labor, Anna and Estusia decided to volunteer for a kommando of workers at a metal factory. Although they told the guards that they were experienced metal workers, they were not. But no one ever checked to see if they were telling the truth. They quickly learned that the factory produced ammunition for the German army.

After she and Estusia were given different jobs and separated, fifteen-year-old Anna observed everything she could about her workroom. She noted that the bathroom had two doors and two sides: one for Jews and one for Germans. She saw what happened to sick or careless workers who were injured; they often disappeared, never to return again. Sometimes the guards made a selection of workers; they, too, never returned. Anna decided to excel at her job, even though she toiled twelve hours a day.

Estusia worked in the powder room, pressing gunpowder into metal pieces. Although she and Anna met at lunch in the factory courtyard, they were not permitted to talk. Anyone who spoke could be beaten or sent away. Still, Anna and Estusia became good friends with some of the other women at the factory.

This led to a brave decision.

The Gunpowder Plot

Early in the summer of 1944, after Anna had been at Auschwitz for about nine months, one of their friends learned that the

Soviet army was close to Warsaw. This meant that the Russians might liberate the camp soon. Their friend believed that the Polish Underground—a secret group of Poles that worked to fight the Nazis—might launch an assault on Auschwitz to free the prisoners.

That news spurred the girls to hatch a plan to help the Underground if it should attack. They began to collect matches, gasoline, and tools to use as weapons. One day, a bold Anna asked a man at the factory for help with their plan:

> I . . . asked him if he could provide me with a pair of insulated wire-cutting shears. We could use them to cut through the electrified wires around the camp. . . . He didn't say a word. . . . One day, he came over and put a box in front of me. . . . I put the box quickly under my chair, but I managed to peek into it. There was a whole loaf of bread inside! I was delighted, but a bit disappointed.[3]

Anna had been expecting to find the wire cutters. Back in the barracks that night with her sister, Anna showed her the bread. When they looked closer, they saw that the wire cutters had been concealed inside. They hid it inside their mattress and told their other friends about their special "present."

One night soon after, a friend named Ala Gertner told the girls that the Sonderkommando in the crematoria would soon

A prewar portrait of Ala Gertner, one of Anna's friends at Auschwitz. Ala helped supply the Sonderkommando with the materials they needed to revolt.

be executed and replaced. The girls realized that they might have to act soon. Anna added the final part of the plan: With Estusia's help, they would steal gunpowder from the factory and give it to the Sonderkommando.

Estusia began passing small amounts of gunpowder to Anna every day. She wrapped them in bits of cloth and placed them in a box. Anna would stop by the powder room and take the box to the garbage bin. She would take the cloth packages from the box and hide them in her dress.

The SS never suspected that the girls would smuggle gunpowder from the factory.

The October 1944 Uprising

On October 7, 1944, the Sonderkommando revolted against the Nazi guards. Using the gunpowder provided by the girls to make grenades and other explosives, they succeeded in destroying Crematorium IV before they were overpowered. All of the Sonderkommando of Crematorium IV were then executed.

The SS suspected that the prisoners who worked at the munitions factory had supplied gunpowder for the revolt. They singled out one young woman who worked at the factory and tortured her. She gave the name of Anna's friend, Ala, as a participant in the plot. After Ala was beaten, she named Estusia and Rózà Robota. Hoping that the three girls would name others, the SS then tortured Estusia, Rózà, and Ala terribly.

Anna was beside herself with fear for her sister's life. Then Anna was called for questioning, but she refused to give any information. A few days later, Estusia and the other two girls were released for a short time. Anna recalled that "Estusia returned, more dead than alive. She was black and blue from head to toe. The skin on her back was broken in stripes. She couldn't move; she couldn't talk."[4]

Then the three were taken into custody again, along with the supervisor of the gunpowder room, Regina Safirztajn.[5] All four were sentenced to death.

On January 5 or 6, 1945, after many delays, they were hanged until dead. Anna was forced to watch the hanging. "I wanted to run," she wrote, but her friends held her tightly. "Suddenly there was a thud of drums, a groan from thousands of throats, and the rest was mist."[6]

Anna was totally defeated after her sister's death:

Anna Heilman (right) and her friend Marta Bindiger walk along a street in Brussels, Belgium, sometime after the war between 1945 and 1947.

> *The day after Estusia's execution . . .*
> *I suddenly realized that the world would go*
> *on without her, that her death wouldn't*
> *make any difference to anybody. I lost my*
> *mind. I became a living corpse; I did not*
> *care if I lived or died.*[7]

One of her surviving friends, Marta Bindiger, helped her through the death march that they were forced to take when the Germans evacuated Auschwitz. When she was freed from another camp on May 2, 1945, she moved first to Belgium, then to Palestine, where she met her husband and had two children. Eventually, she and her family moved to Canada. There, she wrote an autobiography about her experiences in Auschwitz, *Never Far Away.*

Jews in Italy had long been accepted members of the community. But in 1938, the Italian government passed strict laws against Jews. Among other restrictions, Jews were no longer allowed to enter universities. Fortunately, Primo Levi had enrolled at a university one year earlier and was allowed to complete his studies to become a chemist.

When the Germans reinstalled Benito Mussolini as the head of the Italian government in September 1943, however, Levi, along with his sister and mother, fled to the hills in northern Italy. There, he was captured on December 13, 1943, and sent to an Italian-controlled detention camp in Fossoli, Italy. When German SS troops arrived in January 1944 to inspect the camp, all of the 650 Jews held there were placed onto twelve train cars and shipped to Auschwitz.

Primo Levi, pictured here in 1948, was deported to Auschwitz in the winter of 1944.

A Terrible Thirst

The night before they were deported, the Jews in the camp prepared for their journey. As Levi wrote in his autobiography:

> And night came, and it was such a night that one knew that human eyes would not witness it and survive. Everyone felt this: not one of the guards, neither Italian nor German, had the courage to come and see what men do when they know they have to die. All took leave from life in the manner which most suited them. Some praying, some deliberately drunk. . . . But the mothers stayed up to prepare the food for the journey with tender care, and washed their children and packed the luggage; and at dawn the barbed wire was full of children's washing hung out in the wind to dry.[1]

Four days later, upon arrival at Auschwitz, Levi and thirty other men were loaded into a truck and taken to the Buna-Monowitz factory complex. Like the others selected with him, he was terribly thirsty, because no one had been given water for the entire journey. The first room the men were placed in had a faucet with a sign that read: *Drinking Water Forbidden.* Even so, he and the other men could not stop themselves from taking a drink of the terrible, swampy liquid.

In short order, they were sheared, given clothing, and tattooed with an identification number. But they were allowed nothing to drink. Waiting for some sign that he could have a drink, Levi saw an icicle hanging out the barracks window. He reached out and broke it, planning on a taste of melting ice. A guard outside grabbed the icicle away from him.

Levi asked why.

The guard told him that there is no "why" here.

At that moment, Levi realized that "in this place everything is forbidden, not for hidden reasons, but because the camp has been created for that purpose. If one wants to live one must learn this quickly and well. . . ."[2]

This is the cap of a uniform issued to prisoners at Auschwitz. Primo Levi, after receiving his uniform and identification tattoo, was in desperate need of water.

Learning to Survive

Levi did learn quickly. At one point, he listed the lessons he had learned about the camp:

> . . . to reply "Jawohl," never to ask questions, always to pretend to understand. We have learnt the value of food; now we also diligently scrape the bottom of the bowl after the ration and we hold it under our chins when we eat bread so as not to lose the crumbs. . . .[3]

What was true, most of all, was the unending hunger. Some prisoners were so hungry that they would sell their shirt for a portion of bread. When the kapo asked what happened to their shirt, they told him that it had been stolen in the washroom. The prisoners knew that the only punishment would be a beating by the kapo; then they would be issued a new shirt. Eventually, the person would sell the shirt for additional food. Others might have their gold fillings extracted so that they could sell them for bread.

Levi also realized that there were two kinds of prisoners: the drowned and the saved. Most were the former: doomed to die in the gas chamber within three months of their arrival. But Levi saw a few other individuals, who made it their life's work in the camp to be one of the saved:

> *One has to fight against the current; to battle every day and every hour against exhaustion, hunger, cold and the resulting inertia; to resist enemies and have no pity for rivals; to sharpen one's wits, build up one's patience, strengthen one's will power.*[4]

The Last Ten Days

As the Russian army approached, most Auschwitz prisoners were evacuated from the camp beginning January 18, 1945, and forced to march to other concentration camps. Prisoners who tried to flee were executed. But a handful of prisoners were allowed to stay in the camp. Among them was Primo Levi.

A week earlier, he had contracted scarlet fever and had been admitted to the KaBe (or *Krankenbau*), the infirmary for sick prisoners. He was placed in a room with ten beds and thirteen other prisoners suffering from scarlet fever, diphtheria, and typhus. He was fortunate in that he was able to have a bed. Learning that the camp was being evacuated, he and the other patients believed that they would all be killed before the Soviet army arrived. Some twenty thousand prisoners were forced to march out of the camp; but eight hundred hospital patients remained behind.[5]

Two weak Hungarian patients in Levi's room decided to get dressed and join the prisoners who were being evacuated.

A view of the Buna-Werke factory, part of the Buna-Monowitz factory complex. Primo Levi toiled in this forced labor complex after he arrived at Auschwitz.

Levi realized that they were too weak to walk far, but they believed that they would be safer if they joined the evacuation. Levi learned later that they had been shot by the SS when they couldn't keep up in the forced march.

The patients who remained behind began to suffer. The heat, the electricity, the food were all gone. Stronger patients went to search for food, eating anything, even rotten potatoes. They melted dirty snow to have drinking water.

It was risky to leave the KaBe because occasional SS troops retreating from the front passed through the camp. Eighteen patients who had explored the abandoned SS living quarters found a store of food. When SS troops discovered them enjoying a meal in the dining hall, they executed them on the spot.

Other patients died from the cold or their failing health. Their bodies froze in their beds. All were starving, and many were delirious with fever. Of the eleven men left in Levi's room, one died during the last ten days before the camp was liberated. But five more died of their illnesses after the Soviets arrived.

As Levi described the last few days,

We lay in a world of death and phantoms. The last trace of civilization had vanished around and inside us. . . . Whoever waits for his neighbor to die in order to take his piece of bread is . . . further from the model of thinking man than the most primitive pigmy or the most vicious sadist.[6]

A Controversial End

Levi returned to Italy after the war and eventually found work in a chemical factory. He also began to write about his experiences at Auschwitz, at first jotting notes, then expanding them into stories. He wrote many autobiographical books and stories about Auschwitz and became one of the most important authors to write about the Holocaust as a survivor.

Child survivors wearing adult-sized prisoner jackets stand behind the barbed-wire fence at Auschwitz after being liberated by the Russians. Primo Levi was not forced on the "death march" because he was in the camp hospital.

He died on April 11, 1987, in Turin, Italy, when he fell from the third-floor landing of his apartment building. Many have wondered if he committed suicide or if he suffered a bout of dizziness. No one is certain. One of his biographers explained his death this way: "Primo Levi's death . . . was a tragedy, but it was not a victory for Auschwitz."[7]

10　Éva Heyman

"**D**ear diary," wrote thirteen-year-old Éva Heyman on March 19, 1944, "you're the luckiest one in the world, because you cannot feel, you cannot know what a terrible thing has happened to us. The Germans have come!"[1]

Just a month earlier on her thirteenth birthday, Éva had begun to keep a diary, recording not only normal daily occurrences but the beginning of Nazi terror in Hungary. A Hungarian Jew born in Nagyvárad (also called Oradea), she had spent the last five years under increasingly stringent laws aimed at restricting the daily life of Jews.

The Death of Márta

The second entry in her diary related the events that had caused her best friend, Márta, to be killed some three years earlier.

One day in 1941, Márta and her parents had been arrested. The Hungarian government had cracked down on Jews who had not been born in Hungary. Éva learned that "tens of thousands of people like Márta and her family had been taken away to Poland in a train, without luggage and without food."[2] Later, Éva found out that Márta and her parents were executed by machine gunners in Poland. This was Éva's first realization that something terrible was happening in the world.

Éva Heyman was thirteen when this picture was taken.

During the next three years, Hungarian authorities placed
more restrictions on Jews. They could no longer work for the
government or be newspaper editors. But when German troops
moved into Hungary in March 1944, even stricter controls were
soon in place. For example, all Hungarian Jews were forced
to wear a four-inch yellow star on their outer garment. Jewish
businesses were taken over. But what upset Éva most was the
day, April 7, 1944, when the police came to take her treasured
red bicycle:

> *Today they came for my bicycle. I almost caused a big drama. . . . My bicycle had a proper license plate, and Grandpa had paid the tax for it. That's how the policeman found it, because it was registered at City Hall. . . . I threw myself on the ground, held on to the back wheel . . . and shouted all sorts of things at the policemen: "Shame on you for taking away a bicycle from a little girl! That's robbery." . . . One of the policemen was very annoyed and said: "All we need is for a Jew girl to put on such a comedy when her bicycle is taken away. No Jew kid is entitled to keep a bicycle anymore. The Jews aren't entitled to bread either."*[3]

Arrested

The loss of the bicycle was bad enough, but a few days later, the police arrested her stepfather. He was escorted to an elementary school where he was detained for a number of days before being released.

On April 30, the Nazis imposed a curfew that said all Jews were only allowed to leave their homes between the hours of 9 and 10 A.M. At all other times, they were forbidden to be away from home. Then news arrived that all Jews would be placed in a ghetto in their town; they were given a list of what they would be allowed to take:

> *My little Diary, from now on I see everything as a dream. . . . We started to pack . . . I know it is not a dream, but I can't believe it. We can also take bed linen, but we don't know when they are coming to take us, so we can't pack the bed linen just yet. . . . My little Diary, I was never so afraid!*[4]

When the police arrived to remove them in early May, Éva wanted to wear a small gold chain that held the key to her diary. When one policeman refused to allow this, she gave him the chain. Then she put her diary key on a velvet ribbon. A truck waiting outside took them to the ghetto located in the old Jewish Quarter of Nagyvárad. The ghetto was essentially an urban prison camp that would be surrounded by a seven-foot wooden fence.

A father and son wearing their Star of David badges in the Debrecen ghetto in Hungary. Éva and her family had to wear the same badge after the Nazi occupation.

Life in the Nagyvárad Ghetto

Éva could not bear to write for the first five days of her captivity. When she finally added an entry on May 10, 1944, her words revealed the horrors of her new life:

I don't even know where to begin writing, because so many awful things have happened since I last wrote in you. First, the fence was finished, and nobody can go out or come in. . . . From today on, dear diary, we're not in a ghetto but in a ghetto camp, and on every house they've pasted a notice which tells exactly what we're not allowed to do. . . . Actually, everything is forbidden, but the most awful thing of all is that the punishment for everything is death. . . . It doesn't actually say that this punishment also applies to children, but I think it does apply to us, too. The gendarmes came into the house and took all the food we brought along from the pantry. . . . Every time I think: This is the end, things couldn't possibly be worse, and then I find out that it's always possible for everything to get worse, and even much much worse. Until now we had food, and now there won't be anything to eat.[5]

A week later, she heard her grandfather say that some people in the ghetto had begun to kill themselves. Even her grandfather had given poison to older people who had requested it.

The End of Éva's Life

On May 29, after three weeks of imprisonment, authorities announced that the ghetto would be partitioned into districts and deportations would begin. The Jews in the ghetto had no idea what their fate would be: Would they stay in Hungary? Would they be sent to Poland?

On May 30, 1944, Éva reported what she had heard about the deportation:

> They forced 80 people in freight cars and they gave them altogether only one bucket of drinking water. But it is still more awful that they are sealing the cars with padlocks. People will surely suffocate in this terrible heat! The gendarme said he truly didn't understand these Jews. Not even the children cried. They were all like sleepwalkers. They got into those cars stiff, without a word.[6]

Then Éva overheard her mother, Ági, talk of an escape plan. Ági realized that anyone in the ghetto hospital might be able to escape deportation, and a plan was set in motion. When the day arrived for her family's deportation, Éva's main concern was to

Like Éva Heyman, many children wrote diaries during the Holocaust. The surviving diaries provide a glimpse into the daily lives of children during that horrible time. Bruna Cases, a child Holocaust survivor, wrote this illustrated diary page in a Swiss refugee camp.

circa cento metri; vi raggiungeremo.„ Noi
duciosi, nei contrabbandieri non sospettando di
nulla, aspettammo un po' più in là: quand'ecco
che sentiamo parlare sommessamente, tendiamo
orecchie; "In che lingua parlano?„ Bisbigliarono
tutti, "In tedesco„ rispose qualcuno, ancora di
più, frugavano i cespugli con una lampadina
tascabile: non ne potevamo più. Eravamo là
accovacciati; fu un miracolo, pensate, eravamo
in undici, e non ci hanno visto! Poco dopo
le voci si erano allontanate; respirammo; non c'era
più pericolo. È vero che si trattava di svizzeri
tedeschi, ma avrebbero potuto rispedirci in Italia.
Per fortuna c'era con noi un certo dottor Segrè.
Egli disse:"Ci hanno traditi, andiamo avanti,
e la caveremo da soli!„ Poco dopo arrivammo
arrivammo a Stabio, evviva! Avevamo trovato la via
buona.

save her diary. She knew that the family's former maid, Mariska, was trying to gain entry to the ghetto; she planned to give Mariska her diary. As she waited for Mariska, Éva wrote:

> Yet, my little Diary, I don't want to die, I still want to live, even if it means that only I remain behind from this entire district. I would wait for the end of the war in a cellar, or in the attic, or any hole, I would, my little Diary . . . only not to be killed, only to be left alive! . . . I can't write any further, my little Diary, I'm crying with tears and I am in a hurry to see Mariska.[7]

Éva Heyman was then transported to KL-Auschwitz, where she disappeared from life.

The End of the Story

What Éva's diary could not mention is that her mother and stepfather did escape from the ghetto hospital with forged documents and made their way to Switzerland. For reasons that remain unclear, Éva could not be saved and was placed on the transport to Auschwitz.

After the war, Éva's mother tried to find out what had happened to her daughter. She discovered that Éva reached Auschwitz on June 6, 1944, and survived there until October 17, 1944, when she was selected for execution. Ági wrote that

AUTHOR'S NOTE: VISITING AUSCHWITZ TODAY

Most of Auschwitz-Birkenau is in ruins today. This is one of the few remaining barracks in the Auschwitz-Birkenau camp.

Today, the Auschwitz-Birkenau Memorial and Museum has over a million visitors each year. In researching this book, I was able to visit the museum myself.

Even after more than fifty years, KL-Auschwitz is still an overwhelming emotional experience. As a visitor to Auschwitz I, I entered the gate that still reads *Arbeit Macht Frei*. I walked through almost all of the original barracks, since most are well preserved. On the walls of each were the arrival photographs of the earliest political prisoners, the Poles. Museum displays in certain barracks show the tons of human hair, the mounds of eyeglasses and crutches, the suitcases, and even the baby buggies that were taken from the victims of the gas chambers. I visited Block 11, its basement and the courtyard with its Black Wall. At the end, I walked into Crematorium I, where so many people were killed. Visitors had placed memorial candles in front of the doorway. Next to the crematorium, the gallows where Rudolf Höss was hanged after the war still stand.

Unlike Auschwitz I, Auschwitz-Birkenau is in ruins. Most of the barracks are gone, but their chimneys rise above the soggy earth.

The day I visited, the temperature was near freezing and snow was blowing across the deserted camp. I passed through the archway known as the death gate through which trainloads of Jews arrived. That day, on the tracks where the trains once stood, visitors left small bouquets of flowers. I walked from the railroad platform around the complete perimeter of the camp; past the remaining barracks; past the collapsed ruins of Crematoria II, III, IV, and V; past the pond into which human ashes were dumped; past the area where Soviet POWs were buried.

It was not an easy walk to take, but it is an important and unforgettable one. Auschwitz is still there, but it stands now as a memorial to all of the prisoners who died there, so that no one will ever forget.

"a good-hearted female doctor" tried to hide Éva from the Nazi doctor making the selection, the notorious Dr. Mengele.

"Now look at you . . ." he reportedly said, "your feet are foul, reeking with puss! Up with you on the truck!"[8]

An eyewitness told Ági that Mengele had pushed Éva onto the truck; then she was taken to the gas chamber.

Later, when Mariska gave the diary to Éva's mother, Ági was wracked by guilt, because she had not been able to save Éva's life. She edited the diary, removing certain parts that perhaps troubled her. Then she arranged to have a shortened version of the diary published. Soon after the book appeared in 1947, Ági committed suicide, a photograph of Éva beside her.[9] The complete diary was never found.

Éva Heyman and more than a million other victims had their lives cut short tragically at Auschwitz. However, they are remembered and memorialized today. In this photograph, bouquets of flowers rest on the train tracks at Auschwitz in honor and memory of the victims.

Timeline

1940

February 21—Auschwitz (Oświęcim) selected as a suitable site for a concentration camp.

April 27—Heinrich Himmler orders concentration camp to be built at Oświęcim.

April 29—Rudolf Höss selected to be commandant of Auschwitz.

April 30—Höss arrives at Auschwitz.

May 5—First thirty prisoners, all German criminals, arrive at the camp.

June 14—First transport of 728 Polish political prisoners arrives at Auschwitz.

Early July—An old bunker is turned into the first crematorium to dispose of prisoners who die of natural causes.

November 22—First executions at Auschwitz take place. Forty Polish prisoners are shot and then cremated in Crematorium I.

1941

January—I. G. Farben Industries decides to build a synthetic rubber factory near Auschwitz.

March 1—Himmler orders Auschwitz I to be enlarged to hold 30,000 prisoners. He also orders an additional camp (Auschwitz-Birkenau) to be built for 100,000 prisoners who would provide the labor for the Farben factory.

April 7—Prisoners begin forced labor at the Farben factory.

September 3—Zyklon B gas first used to kill 600 Russian and 250 camp hospital prisoners in the basement of Block 11 at Auschwitz.

October—The Nazis begin using Soviet prisoners to build Auschwitz-Birkenau about two miles from Auschwitz I.

1942

February 15—The first known transport of Jews (from Bytom, Germany) arrives at Auschwitz I. All are killed with Zyklon B gas in Crematorium I.

March—First gas chamber (Bunker 1, sometimes called "the Little Red House") goes into operation at Auschwitz-Birkenau.

Summer—Second gas chamber (Bunker 2, sometimes called "the Little White House") goes into operation at Auschwitz-Birkenau.

December 16—Himmler orders the deportation of all Roma living in Germany and Austria, as well as Bohemia and Moravia, to Auschwitz.

1943

February 26—The first transport of Roma from Germany arrives at Auschwitz and the "Gypsy Camp" is begun at Auschwitz II.

March to June—Four larger crematoria (II, III, IV, and V) are constructed at Auschwitz-Birkenau for the execution of increasing number of Jewish transports.

March 13—Most of a transport of Jews from the Krakow ghetto are gassed in Crematorium II at Auschwitz-Birkenau as a test of the new facility.

March 22—Crematorium IV placed into operation.

March 31—Crematorium II placed into operation.

April 4—Crematorium V placed into operation.

May—Dr. Josef Mengele arrives at Auschwitz where he conducts inhumane experiments on prisoners.

June 25—Crematorium III placed into operation.

1944

May 2—The first two transports of Hungarian Jews arrive in Auschwitz.

August 2—The "Gypsy Camp" at Auschwitz II is liquidated; some three thousand Roma are sent to the gas chamber.

October 7—Hundreds of Sonderkommando assigned to Crematorium IV revolt at Auschwitz-Birkenau.

November 25—Himmler orders the destruction of the crematoria at Auschwitz II.

1945

January 18—Nazis evacuate Auschwitz, forcing many prisoners on a "death march."

January 27—First Soviet soldiers enter Auschwitz and liberate the remaining prisoners.

1947

April 16—Rudolf Höss is executed at Auschwitz.

July 2—Auschwitz Museum is created.

Chapter Notes

Introduction

1. Olga Lengyel, *Five Chimneys: A Woman Survivor's True Story of Auschwitz* (Chicago: Academy Chicago Publishers, 1995), p. 6.
2. Ibid., p. 9.
3. Ibid., p. 8.
4. Ibid., p. 15.
5. Teresa and Henryk Swiebocki, *Auschwitz: The Residence of Death*, 6th ed., trans. William Brand (Krakow- Oświęcim, Poland: Bialy Kruk, 2007), p. 8.
6. Laurence Rees, *Auschwitz: A New History* (New York: Public Affairs, 2005), p. 19.
7. Yisrael Gutman, "Auschwitz—An Overview," in Yisrael Gutman and Michael Berenbaum, *Anatomy of the Auschwitz Death Camp* (Bloomington, Ind.: Indiana University Press, 1998), p. 16.
8. Rudolf Höss, *Death Dealer: The Memoirs of the SS Kommandant at Auschwitz*, ed. Steven Paskuly (New York: Da Capo Press, 1996), p. 156.
9. Franciszek Piper, "The Mass Extermination of Jews in the Gas Chambers," in *Auschwitz: Nazi Death Camp* (Oświęcim, Poland: Auschwitz-Birkenau State Museum, 2004), p. 166.
10. Ibid., p. 170
11. Swiebocki, p. 11.
12. "Bunker No. 1," Memorial and Museum Auschwitz-Birkenau, n.d., <http://www.auschwitz.org.pl/new/index.php?language=EN&tryb=stale&id=371> (September 16, 2008).
13. Piper, p. 167.
14. "Bunker No. 2," Memorial and Museum Auschwitz-Birkenau, n.d., <http://www.auschwitz.org.pl/new/index.php?language=EN&tryb=stale&id=365> (September 16, 2008).
15. Rees, p. 169.
16. Franciszek Piper, "Prisoner Labor," in *Auschwitz: Nazi Death Camp*, Franciszek Piper and Teresa Swiebocka, eds. (Oświęcim, Poland: Auschwitz-Birkenau State Museum, 2004), p. 109.
17. Rees, p. 171.
18. Ibid.
19. Jean-Claude Pressac with Robert-John van Pelt, "The Machinery of Mass Murder at Auschwitz," in Yisrael Gutman and Michael Berenbaum, *Anatomy of the Auschwitz Death Camp* (Bloomington, Ind.: Indiana University Press, 1998), p. 239.

20. Franciszek Piper, "The Number of Victims at KL Auschwitz," in *Auschwitz: Nazi Death Camp*, p. 194.
21. Ibid., p. 195

Chapter 1. Kazimierz Albin

1. Kazimierz Albin, *Warrant of Arrest* (Oświęcim, Poland: The Auschwitz-Birkenau State Museum, 2003), pp. 58–59.
2. Ibid., p. 59.
3. Ibid., p. 61.
4. Danuta Czech, "The Auschwitz Prisoner Administration," in Yisrael Gutman and Michael Berenbaum, *Anatomy of the Auschwitz Death Camp* (Bloomington, Ind.: Indiana University Press, 1998), p. 364.
5. Debórah Dwork and Robert Jan van Pelt, *Auschwitz: 1270 to the Present* (New York: Norton, 1996), p. 232.
6. Czech, p. 366.
7. Albin, p. 66.
8. Ibid., p. 68.
9. Ibid., p. 79.
10. Ibid., p. 184.

Chapter 2. Rudolf Höss

1. Rudolf Höss, *Death Dealer: The Memoirs of the SS Kommandant at Auschwitz*, ed. Steven Paskuly (New York: Da Capo Press, 1996), p. 153.
2. Ibid., p. 59.
3. Ibid., p. 201.
4. Ibid., p. 96.
5. Ibid., p. 100.
6. Ibid., p. 118.
7. "The 64th Anniversary of the Opening of the Auschwitz Camp for Soviet POWs," Memorial and Museum Auschwitz-Birkenau, n.d., <http://en.auschwitz.org.pl/m/index.php?option=com_content&task=view&id=438&Itemid=8> (September 27, 2008).
8. Höss, pp. 156–157.
9. "Extract From Written Evidence of Rudolf Höss, Commander of the Auschwitz Extermination Camp," Yad Vashem, The Holocaust Martyrs' and Heroes' Remembrance Authority, Documents of the Holocaust Part 2, n.d., <http://www1.yadvashem.org/about_holocaust/documents/part2/doc164.html> (September 17, 2008).
10. Debórah Dwork and Robert Jan van Pelt, *Auschwitz: 1270 to the Present* (New York: Norton, 1996), p. 96.
11. Ibid., p. 290.
12 Höss, p. 27.
13. Ibid., p. 28.
14. Ibid., pp. 158–159.

15. Ibid., p. 162.
16. Ibid., p. 189.
17. Laurence Rees, *Auschwitz: A New History* (New York: Public Affairs, 2005), p. 289.

Chapter 3. **Pery Broad**

1. Pery Broad, *Reminiscences of Pery Broad, in KL Auschwitz Seen by the SS*, trans. Krystyna Michalik (Oświęcim, Poland: The Auschwitz-Birkenau State Museum, 2007), p. 110.
2. Ibid., pp. 110–111.
3. Robert Jan van Pelt, "A Site in Search of a Mission," in Yisrael Gutman and Michael Berenbaum, *Anatomy of the Auschwitz Death Camp* (Bloomington, Ind.: Indiana University Press, 1998), p. 145.
4. Ibid., pp. 129–130.
5. Ibid., p. 130.
6. Debórah Dwork and Robert Jan van Pelt, *Auschwitz: 1270 to the Present* (New York: Norton, 1996), p. 219.
7. Andrey Pogozhev, *Escape From Auschwitz* (Barnsley, UK: Pen & Sword, 2007), pp. 54–55.
8. Laurence Rees, *Auschwitz: A New History* (New York: Public Affairs, 2005), p. 54.
9. Jean-Claude Pressac with Robert-John van Pelt, "The Machinery of Mass Murder at Auschwitz," in Yisrael Gutman and Michael Berenbaum, *Anatomy of the Auschwitz Death Camp* (Bloomington, Ind.: Indiana University Press, 1998), p. 215.
10. Broad, p. 105.
11. Ibid., p. 125.
12. Ibid., p. 146.
13. Hermann Langbein, *People in Auschwitz*, trans. Harry Zohn (Chapel Hill; N.C.: University of North Carolina Press, 2003), p. 389.
14. Ibid.
15. Jerzy Rawicz, "Foreword," in *KL Auschwitz Seen by the SS*, trans. Krystyna Michalik (Oświęcim, Poland: The Auschwitz-Birkenau State Museum, 2007), p. 9.

Chapter 4. **Andrey Pogozhev**

1. Andrey Pogozhev, *Escape From Auschwitz* (Barnsley, U.K.: Pen & Sword, 2007), p. 20.
2. Ibid., p. 21.
3. Ibid., p. 23.
4. Ibid., p. 50.
5. Ibid., p. 65.
6. Ibid., p. 68.
7. Ibid., p. 105.
8. Ibid., p. 155.

9. Ibid., p. 159.
10. Ibid., p. 162.
11. Rebecca Wittmann, *Beyond Justice: The Auschwitz Trial* (Cambridge, Mass.: Harvard University Press, 2008), p. 285.

Chapter 5. **Walter Winter**

1. Walter Winter, *Winter Time: Memoirs of a German Sinto who Survived Auschwitz*, trans. Struan Robertson (Hatfield, UK: University of Hertfordshire Press, 2004), p. 11.
2. Ibid., p. 24.
3. Ibid., p. 36.
4. Toby Sonneman, *Shared Sorrows: A Gypsy Family Remembers the Holocaust* (Hatfield, U.K.: University of Hertfordshire Press, 2002), p. 31.
5. Romani Rose, ed., *The National Socialist Genocide of the Sinti and Roma*, Catalogue of the permanent exhibition in the State Museum of Auschwitz (Heidelberg, Germany: Dokumentations- und Kulturzentrum Deutscher Sinti und Roma, 2003), p. 213.
6. Winter, p. 45.
7. Ibid., p. 49.
8. Yehuda Bauer, "Gypsies," in Yisrael Gutman and Michael Berenbaum, *Anatomy of the Auschwitz Death Camp* (Bloomington, Ind.: Indiana University Press, 1998), p. 448.
9. Winter, p. 81.
10. Ibid., p. 83.
11. Ibid., p. 84.
12. Bauer, p. 449.
13. Winter, p. 137.
14. Laurence Rees, *Auschwitz: A New History* (New York: Public Affairs, 2005), p. 248.
15. Bauer, p. 450.
16. Winter, pp. 122–123.

Chapter 6. **Dr. Miklos Nyiszli**

1. "Hungary before the German Occupation," United States Holocaust Memorial Museum (USHMM), n.d., <http://www.ushmm.org/wlc/article.php?ModuleId=10005457> (September 3, 2008).
2. Miklos Nyiszli, *Auschwitz: A Doctor's Eyewitness Account*, trans. Tibère Kremer and Richard Seaver (New York: Arcade Publishing, 1993), pp. 51–52.
3. Ibid., p. 115.
4. Ibid., p. 54.
5. Andrezej Strzelecki, "The Plunder of Victims and Their Corpses," in Yisrael Gutman and Michael Berenbaum, *Anatomy of the Auschwitz Death Camp* (Bloomington, Ind.: Indiana University Press, 1998), p. 259.

6. Ibid., pp. 260.
7. Nyiszli, p. 120.
8. Ibid., p. 177.
9. Ibid., p. 181.
10. Ibid., p. 222.

Chapter 7. **Shlomo Dragon**

1. Gideon Greif, *We Wept Without Tears: Testimonies from the Jewish Sonderkommando from Auschwitz* (New Haven, Conn.: Yale University Press, 2005), p. 128.
2. Ibid., p. 133.
3. Ibid.
4. Ibid., p. 4.
5. Ibid., pp. 153–155.
6. Ibid., p. 169.
7. Ibid., p. 43.
8. Ibid.
9. Barbara Jarosz, "Organization of the Camp Resistance Movement and Their Activities" in *Auschwitz: Nazi Death Camp*, eds. Franciszek Piper and Teresa Swiebocka (Oświęcim, Poland: Auschwitz-Birkenau State Museum, 2004), p. 233.
10. Greif, p. 177.
11. Ibid., p. 179.
12. Gideon Greif and Andreas Kilian, "Significance, Responsibility, Challenge: Interviewing the Sonderkommando Survivors" Sonderkommando-Studien, April 7, 2004, <http://www.sonderkommando-studien.de/artikel. php?c=forschung/significance> (September 25, 2008).

Chapter 8. **Anna Heilman**

1. Anna Heilman, *Never Far Away: The Auschwitz Chronicles of Anna Heilman* (Calgary: University of Calgary Press, 2001), p. 80.
2. Ibid., pp. 82–83.
3. Ibid., p. 126.
4. Ibid., p. 132.
5. Ibid.
6. Ibid., p. 140.
7. Ibid.

Chapter 9. **Primo Levi**

1. Primo Levi, *Survival in Auschwitz: The Nazi Assault on Humanity*, trans. Stuart Woolf (New York: Touchstone, 1996), p. 15.
2. Ibid., p. 29.
3. Ibid., p. 33.

4. Ibid., p. 92.
5. Ibid., pp. 155–156.
6. Ibid., pp. 171–172.
7. Carole Angier, *The Double Bond: The Life of Primo Levi* (New York: Farrar, Straus, and Giroux, 2002), p. 727.

Chapter 10. Éva Heyman

1. "Dear Diary, I Don't Want to Die," Yad Vashem Education Ceremony, n.d., <http://www1.yadvashem.org/education/ceremonie/english/Jenuary2006/January2006.htm#005> (September 21, 2008).
2. "Éva Heyman on the Deporting of her friend, Marta, from Hungary," Shoah Resource Center, Yad Vashem, n.d., <http://www1.yadvashem.org/odot_pdf/Microsoft%20Word%20-%203689.pdf> (September 21, 2008).
3. Jacob Boas, ed., *We Are Witnesses: Five Diaries of Teenagers Who Died in the Holocaust* (New York: Henry Holt, 1995), pp. 130–131.
4. "Extracts from the Diary of Éva Heyman," trans. by Susan Geroe, The Yizkor Book Project, The Agony of the Oradea Jewry, n.d., <http://www.jewishgen.org/yizkor/oradea/oradea320.html> (September 21, 2008).
5. "Éva Heyman on the Hardships of the Ghetto," Shoah Resource Center, Yad Vashem, n.d., <http://www1.yadvashem.org/odot_pdf/Microsoft%20Word%20-%203697.pdf > (September 21, 2008).
6. The Yizkor Book Project.
7. Ibid.
8. Boas, p. 152.
9. Ibid., p. 153.

Permissions

Glossary

Arbeit Macht Frei—German phrase found above the main gate of Auschwitz I. It means "Work will make you free."

"Aryan"—A term misused by the Nazis to indicate the racially pure race of true Germans.

crematorium—A building where bodies are burned, or cremated.

ghetto—Part of a city or town where Jews were forcibly segregated by the Germans or other authorities.

kapo—A prisoner in charge of a work party.

kommando—A work party.

konzentrationslager—Concentration camp (German), sometimes abbreviated KL.

krankenbau—Prisoner's hospital (German).

pathology—The branch of medical science that studies the causes, nature, and effects of diseases.

Sonderkommando—Special work group assigned to the gas chambers and crematoria (German).

SS—Short for *Schutzstaffel*, or "Protective Squadron" in German, a police and military organization that was highly loyal to Adolf Hitler. Among other duties, the SS provided the supervision of the concentration camps. As a result, the SS committed most of the German war crimes during World War II.

typhus—An infectious disease spread by lice that can cause death, especially in older people, if left untreated.

Further Reading

Books

Boraks-Nemetz, Lilian, and Irene N. Watts, eds. *Tapestry of Hope: Holocaust Writing for Young People*. Plattsburg, N.Y.: Tundra Books of Northern New York, 2003.

Downing, David. *The Nazi Death Camps*. Milwaukee, Wis.: World Almanac Library, 2006.

Lawton, Clive A. *Auschwitz: The Story of a Nazi Death Camp*. Cambridge, Mass.: Candlewick, 2002.

Lee, Carol Ann. *Anne Frank and the Children of the Holocaust*. New York: Puffin, 2008.

Levine, Karen. *Hana's Suitcase: A True Story*. Morton Grove, Ill.: Albert Whitman, 2003.

Pressburger, Chava, ed. *The Diary of Petr Ginz*. Trans. Elena Lappin. New York: Atlantic Monthly Press, 2007.

Robson, David. *Auschwitz*. Detroit: Lucent Books, 2009.

Internet Addresses

Auschwitz: Inside the Nazi State (PBS)
<http://www.pbs.org/auschwitz/>

Memorial and Museum, Auschwitz-Birkenau
<http://en.auschwitz.org.pl/m/>

Yad Vashem—The Auschwitz Album
<http://www1.yadvashem.org/exhibitions/album_auschwitz/index.html>

Index